ACROSS THE OCEAN

OCEAN

A Memoir

CHRISTOPHER DO

ISBN: 9798480431018

This book is dedicated to the loving memories of my father, Victor Do and my mother, Ty Hoang.

∞∞∞∞

With special thanks to my wife Michelle, who put up with me for staying up late every night writing, and to my daughters Nikki and Courtney, who continue to inspire me to look at the world through open mind.

The best things in life come in three, like friends, dreams, and memories.

  -   *Mencius*

.

It is only with the heart that one can see rightly; what is essential is invisible to the eye.

  -   *Antoine de Saint-Exupéry*

ACROSS THE OCEAN

CONTENTS

PREFACE

I had wanted to write a book for a long time but did not know how to get started. The idea of writing a book came from some of my former colleagues at USCIS who encouraged me to write about my journey to America. At first, it did not occur to me that my story would be worth writing since there were thousands of people who also came to America at the end of the Vietnam War, and thousands more came after the war during the late seventies through the early nineties. Many books had been written about the harrowing tales of the boat people, and hundreds of thousands of people had perished in the open sea. My story would be pale compared to those stories. When I retired a few years ago, the idea came back to me, and I wanted to write a book to tell my story to my family and friends, but I did not want it to be only about my journey to America. I also wanted to write about my childhood memories, the war from my perspective as someone who grew up during the turbulent time in Vietnam, and about starting a new life in America. Most importantly, I wanted my book to be a legacy which I could pass on to my family.

When the pandemic hit the U.S. in early 2020, we

were very much confined inside of our home, and I
thought this would be the best opportunity for me to
reflect on my life, and work on the book that I had long
wanted to write. Still, the idea of writing a book seemed to
be a daunting task. The good news was since I retired, I
wrote and posted several stories to Facebook, so I could
start with those by rewriting and adding to them. The next
step for me was to decide whether I should write the book
in Vietnamese or in English. Since I never wrote a book
before, I decided to start easy first by writing it in my
native language, just so I could go through the process of
writing, editing, formatting and rewriting to see how it
goes. To see the fruit of my hard work alone was
satisfactory enough for me. When I got my book printed
and I sent copies to my family and friends last year, I
received much positive feedback. That had encouraged
me to work on the English version of the book.

As I was working on my second book, the number
of Covid cases in the U.S. kept getting higher and higher.
By November 2020, the total number of cases had
surpassed ten million, with an average of over 100,000
new cases a day, and the total number of deaths passed
300,000. When we got together with our immediate
family for Thanksgiving, I told my family we were
thankful that no one in our family, including our
extended families, had been infected with the virus. In
January 2021, I felt optimistic that we had a new
administration, and a new president who made stopping
the pandemic his top priority, and that we also had two
Covid vaccines approved for emergency use by the FDA.
Finally, we started to see light at the end of the tunnel.
Then, we learned of devastating news that my father and

my sister Thu had tested positive for Covid. They both had Covid symptoms such as fever, fatigue, and diarrhea.

After two weeks, my sister, who had Covid-induced pneumonia, was getting better, and my father also seemed to do better since his situation was less severe. A week later, however, my father complained he felt his tongue was burning, and he could not taste, and smell anything. I could feel that he was also getting weaker because he could not eat much. We called the ambulance to take him to the hospital out of precaution; the doctors kept him overnight then sent him home the next day. They said his numbers were normal and suggested we followed up with an ENT specialist regarding his tongue problem. But two days later, his condition took a turn for the worse, and he passed away because of complications affecting his lungs and kidneys.

We were all shocked and saddened as we thought he was getting better, and also because we could not say goodbye to him as appropriately as we would under normal circumstances. I kept asking myself the question: how did the U.S.–one of the richest and most powerful countries get to this point?

When the first case was reported in early January 2020 in Washington state, and even when the numbers jumped to millions of cases, I would never have imagined that it could happen to our family; we were careful and followed the CDC guidelines religiously. My father also wore his mask everywhere he went, but he was also a stubborn man who refused to stay indoors for extended periods. That was probably how he got infected with the virus and passed it on to my sister. Our daughter Nikki told me perhaps I had said it too soon when I said the thankful prayer for Thanksgiving.

By mid-January 2021, the U.S. had reached a grim milestone as the newly elected president Joe Biden held vigil for 400,000 lives lost to Covid-19 in the U.S. Four hundred candlelights illuminated the Lincoln Memorial Reflecting Pool to remember those who died - one candle for every thousand lives lost. At home, we also lit a candle for our dad and for all those people who died of the virus. I felt that hundreds of thousands of lives in the U.S., and perhaps around the world, would have been saved if the previous president did not lie about the virus, and took the appropriate actions to prevent the virus from spreading everywhere.

After our father's passing, it took me a while to collect myself emotionally and start working on my book again. I wanted to finish the book as a dedication to him and also to my mother. I was glad that my father could read my first book I sent to him on his 93rd birthday in November, although we could not gather and celebrate with him as we normally do every year.

I also wanted to assert that some stories in my book about the Vietnam War, as well as past and current politics, are based on my perspective and research, and therefore are unavoidably incomplete, but nonetheless they are my humble and honest attempt to explain history.

This book is not a direct translation of my previous book from Vietnamese to English, but rather it is almost a complete rewrite with some stories combined and/or removed and new ones added.

Vigil at Lincoln Memorial Reflecting Pool to honor 400,000
lives lost to Covid-19 on January 19, 2021
(Source: The Guardian)

THE SCHOOL YEARS

To this day, I still do not know why my grandfather chose me for enrollment in a French school system when I became of school age in the early sixties. He did not choose any of my other siblings, and I was not even the oldest nor the youngest child, for that matter. French schools in Saigon at the time were reserved for people with privileges - children of French diplomats and French businessmen who lived and worked in Saigon, and the wealthy Vietnamese families who could afford to pay for their children to go there. You see, my father worked as a clerk at the "Banque de l'Indochine" back then, and there was no way he could pay the tuition for me to attend a private French school with his salary. I should feel special and grateful, but somehow, I always felt guilty because I was favored over my siblings. That feeling of guilt only ceased when I quit French school years later and attended regular school during my high school years.

I had started kindergarten at Chi-Lan, a local school

near our house, but the next year my grandfather enrolled me in first grade at Lamartine, a French elementary school in downtown Saigon. The school was named after Alphonse de Lamartine, a French author and poet from the 19th century. Every morning when the sun was not yet up and the chilly breeze was still in the air, my mother got up early to walk me to the bus stop, which was a long walk along a dirt road. Those images leave a fond memory of her in my mind every time I read the opening paragraph of the book "I Go to School" from the well-known Vietnamese author Thanh-Tinh. In those moments, I wish I could travel back in time so I could hold her hand once again as we walk along that dirt road of my childhood. Thanh-Tinh wrote:

"The early dawn of that morning, a morning filled with autumn air and cold breeze. My mother gently held my hand and walked me down the long and narrow road. This road I had traveled many times before, but this time I felt so different. The surrounding images had all changed for inside me, there was a big change: Today, I go to school." [1]

I should mention that my grandfather was not really a wealthy man. He was a civil servant and mayor of Hanoi in 1952 until he was dismissed in 1954 for collaborating with the French in evacuating anti-communists.[2] After the Geneva Accord was signed, he moved to the South with his family. My grandfather was a patriot and a staunch nationalist who opposed the French colonial rule. However, he despised the Hanoi communist government more, because they killed three of his sons during their bloody suppression of the Vietnam Nationalist Party in 1946.

After World War II ended in 1945, the allied powers at Potsdam had decided that the Chinese nationalist army under Chiang Kai-shek would disarm the Japanese troops stationed north of the 16th latitude in Vietnam, and the British forces under Lord Mountbatten would disarm the Japanese troops stationed south of 16th latitude. The British, however, invited France back to Indochina and turned authority over to the French. Meanwhile, the Viet Minh quickly took advantage of the situation to seize power from the Tran Trong Kim government, and declared Vietnam as an independent state. Their leader, Ho Chi Minh, then methodically eliminated his opponents, including leaders of the non-communist parties, to consolidate power.

In 1946, Ho made a deal with France to let the French forces return to the North to replace General Lu Han's Chinese troops. With the Chinese nationalist troops out of Vietnam, Ho's hand was free to purge and murder many of the Vietnam Nationalist Party members, including my grandfather's three sons. Hostilities between the French and the Viet Minh continued, and finally war broke out between the Viet Minh and the French, marking the beginning of the first Indochina War.[3] This led to the defeat of France at Dien Bien Phu in 1954, and eventually the Geneva Accord in July of the same year. The Accord was signed by the Democratic Republic of Vietnam (Viet Minh), France, the People's Republic of China, the Soviet Union and the United Kingdom.

Following the provisions of the Geneva Accord, Vietnam would be temporarily divided along the 17th

Parallel, French Union forces would regroup to the south of the line and Viet Minh to the north, free movement of the population between the zones would be allowed for three hundred days, and free general elections would be held two years later in July 1956 to reunite the country. The general election would be under the supervision of the International Control Commission (ICC) comprising Canada, Poland and India. [4] It was during this period that my grandparents and my parents, including everyone in the family along with more than a million people in the North, chose freedom and migrated to the South in the same year.

In the South, the U.S. replaced the French as the political power and backed up Ngo Dinh Diem, the Prime Minister of the State of Vietnam. In 1955, Diem defeated emperor Bao Dai in a government-controlled referendum and proclaimed himself the president of the first Republic of Vietnam. Diem then forced France to withdraw from Vietnam. The last French forces left Vietnam in April 1956.

Citing the reason that it was impossible for the people in the North to have a fair and free election, Diem refused to hold the general election planned for 1956. He also claimed that the South did not sign and therefore was not bound to the Geneva Accord. North Vietnam responded by refusing to withdraw all Viet Minh troops from South Vietnam and conducting military buildup to increase the number of its armed divisions in the South. The U.S. began to support the Army of the Republic of Vietnam (ARVN) which was created as a replacement for the Vietnamese National Army. Hence, the beginning of the second Indochina War, or Vietnam War.

During the period from 1954 to 1963, life in South Vietnam under the first republic was peaceful and prosperous. In 1963, however, there were signs of trouble as Buddhist protests, incited by communist agents, spread across Saigon and at the ancient capital Huế.[5]

In November 1963, our elementary school, Lamartine, was destroyed during the coup d'état to overthrow the South Vietnam government of Ngo Dinh Diem because of its proximity to the Cong Hoa garrison. The government forces had set up defense there to protect the presidential palace, but it was annihilated along with our school. After the coup, we moved to Colette, a French elementary school for girls also in downtown Saigon. The school was known for its red painted walls and stood out at the corner of Le Van Duyet and Ho Xuan Huong streets. It was located right near where Thich Quang Duc, a Buddhist monk, infamously burned himself to death to protest against President Diem's regime approximately five months before the coup. According to some witnesses, the monk appeared to be drugged before committing self-immolation to create a public outcry and negate the U.S. support of President Diem.[6] The event was one of the major factors that led to the overthrow of his government and eventually the murder of Diem and his brother.

Mark Moyar, in his book "Triumph Forsaken", wrote that when Ho Chi Minh learned of the assassination of Diem, Ho said, "I can scarcely believe that the Americans would be so stupid." Moyar wrote that the pro-communist Australian Wilfred Burchett, who spent time with the Vietnamese communist leaders after the coup, told an American journalist in 1964 that they

5

were amazed by the event and believed it was a gift to them. They exclaimed, "The Americans have done something that we haven't been able to do for nine years, and that was get rid of Diem."

During my elementary school years, I was a good student and was always among the top of my classes. Every year I received "tableau d'honneur" (certificate of award.) At the end of the year near Christmas, we cut green colored papers to make Christmas trees, and we sang Christmas carols in French.

In the following years, Saigon was in a state of unrest with many crises. The generals, after overthrowing the government at the direction of Ambassador Cabot Lodge, were fighting among each other to seize power for themselves. There were demonstrations from the Buddhists and college students demanding changes almost daily. The police and security forces were deployed throughout the capital city to crush the demonstrations. Sometimes tear gas fired by the police flew into the classrooms. Our teacher had to close all the windows and doors, but still the tear gas would make us rub our eyes and wipe our tears in vain.

Every year, the school conducted physical exams for all students, but ever since the boys arrived, the school staff had to plan to dó the check-up for all the boys and girls in a separate and orderly fashion. We were told to sit in two separate waiting rooms in the *infirmerie* with our clothes off and wait for our names to be called before entering the exam room.

One year, while I was waiting with the boys in our room, I heard my name called, so I opened the door and walked into the exam room. Almost instantly, the door from the girls' waiting room also opened, and a girl walked in. We were both shocked and embarrassed since we were both completely naked. Just when we did not know what to do, an old French nurse yelled at me to get out. It turned out that the girl's name rhymed with mine, and when the French nurse called her name from afar in the exam room, it caused the confusion on my part.

The physical exams got a little better when we got older, as we could keep our underwear on, but we had to wait in line half-naked in the schoolyard in front of the *infirmerie*. It was awkward nevertheless, since we had a new and younger nurse. During the check-up, the nurse would tell us to drop our underwear so she could check our private parts. We heard a rumor that when one boy got a little too anxious; he was punished and sent to detention for a couple hours after school. That really got all of us freaked out, but somehow, we managed to survive the affair.

At the beginning of our fifth grade, we were transferred to St. Exupéry. The school was also painted with the red color and near the intersection of Doan Thi Diem and Ngo Thoi Nhiem. At that time, my father bought me a bicycle, and I would ride it to school every day. In front of the school, there was a Chinese man who made the perfect fried flour cakes, and I was so addicted to it I ate there almost every day after school. The flour cakes were cut into finger size pieces and fried over a large pan until they were slightly brown, which the man then sprayed with soy sauce and hot sauce as he continued to fry them until they became sizzling with an orange-red color. He then served the flour cakes on a small round plate sprinkled with chopped green onions on top, and when I had some extra money, he would throw in a fried egg. Decades later, I went to many places in different Chinatowns in the U.S. but I could never find the same taste of the fried flour cakes from those yesteryears.

In 1968, during the Tet Offensive, the front building of St. Exupéry was severely damaged with arrays of bullet holes. The attack began early morning on New Year's Day of the Vietnamese Tet holiday when the communists violated the truce and launched a surprise coordinated attack across all major cities and towns in South Vietnam. In Saigon, we were celebrating the lunar new year. The sound of firecrackers exploded everywhere, but then suddenly, it sounded more like gunfire and we found out that the capital was under attack.

The attacks went on for several months. All schools in Saigon were closed during this period. When everyone thought it was over, we all went back to school, and then the Viet Cong launched the second wave of attack, and the schools were closed again. The wave of smaller scale attacks occurred sporadically throughout the year. The destruction was everywhere and the human casualties were horrific. I have never forgotten the images that were shown over and over on national TV of the mass graves discovered many months after the attack in the city of Huế. Thousands of people, including civilians, were found bound together and executed by the Viet Cong during their short occupation there in the ancient capital.[7]

In Saigon, AP photographer Eddie Adams captured the brutality of the war in a still photograph of South Vietnamese General Nguyen Ngoc Loan executing a Viet Cong captain on February 1, 1968. The picture quickly flashed around the world and helped shape American public opinion against the war. What the picture did not show was before his execution, the Viet Cong captain and his death squad had murdered a dozen of unarmed civilians, including the entire family but a nine-year-old boy of an armor officer in the Army of the Republic of Vietnam. The boy was shot in the head, but somehow, survived.

Little did I know, fifteen years later, the young system engineer I worked with at a defense company in Virginia was that little boy who survived the massacre of his family in 1968. I remember I was working on a research project for my Master's degree at George Mason University and needed a computer to run my program; he helped me to build my first personal computer (PC) which was called PC XT. The system engineer, H. T. Nguyen, never spoke about his family tragedy, later joined the U.S. Navy in 1991, and eventually became the first Vietnamese American rear admiral of the U.S. Navy in 2019. I only found out about his story after I read it in the news in 2019.

As for the general, the execution changed his life. He was relieved of his command after he was severely wounded three months later during a battle against the Viet Cong in Saigon. He was taken to Australia for treatment, but there was a strong public outcry against him there, and he was moved to Walter Reed Army Medical Center in Washington, D.C. After the fall of Saigon, he came to the U.S. and settled in Northern Virginia. There were unsuccessful efforts to deport him as a war criminal in 1978. He ran a pizza restaurant in the suburb of Burke, but had to retire after he received threats from the people who recognized him. After retirement, he lived quietly, and died of cancer in 1998. He was 67 years old.

Eddie Adams' photo won a Pulitzer Prize, but he later regretted taking the picture. In 2001, he wrote in Time Magazine: "The general killed the Viet Cong; I killed the general with my camera." The photo actually killed a country, as I believe it had changed the course of the Vietnam War.

Back in school in 1968, we never talked about the attack. Perhaps because we were still too young to understand what happened. After all, it was the longest school break we ever had. During the following months, the Viet Cong resorted to terrorist tactics to terrorize the capital city. The communists used Russian-made 122 mm rockets and portable launchers to fire indiscriminately into Saigon. Life Magazine on June 28, 1968 reported: "Firing from hideouts in swamp and jungle up to seven miles away, the enemy has been pouring a barrage of rockets on the city. The rockets, 'whispering death', the Saigonese call them - fall in chillingly haphazard pattern." These attacks were nerve-racking since they always came randomly, unannounced, during the still of the night, thus when you went to bed at night, you would not know whether you would wake up the next morning. It was terrifying for the people in the city, let alone a child of my age.

Bunker buildings with sandbags inside people's homes became a big business, although it did not really give you real protection, since by the time you heard the rocket coming, it was already too late, unless, of course, if the whole family could sleep in it the whole night. My grandfather had a bunker built in one room downstairs in his house. One night, I was sleeping over at his house in the bedroom upstairs; I heard a loud whistling noise, and when I looked up outside of the window, I saw a ball of fire whizzing by, and then I heard an enormous explosion. The explosion shook the house as if a train had just run by it. After the shaking stopped, there was just total silence, deadly silence. For the first time, I could truly understand the meaning of the lyrics in the song "The Sound of Silence" because for the first time, I could hear the deadly silence. It happened so fast, and by the time it was over, I did not even have time to run downstairs to go into the bunker. I just lay there in the bed, still shaking from the explosion.

After a while, I went downstairs, and I saw my grandfather and other people in the neighborhood wandering outside to see where the rocket had landed. I followed them out, and the first thing I noticed was the smell, the smell of explosives like burning rubber mixing with flesh. The rocket had barely missed my grandparent's house, and hit a row of houses across the street. I saw a man carry a little girl out in his arms from the rubble, red blood soaked her white pajamas and her tiny body. That image had haunted me ever since. The Saigon government and the U.S. military command promised to stop these attacks, but stopping them proved to be a challenge. The communists used small units comprising only two-person teams to fire the rockets with a launcher mounted on a makeshift tripod, and then they moved to a different location for the next target. By the time a helicopter went up to look for them, they were already gone. According to Life Magazine, the military had to send troops out frequently to sweep the area for thirty miles around the city, and set up triple rings of mine fields reinforced with sophisticated electronic gear to stop them.

During the school year 1968-69, I went to Lycée Jean Jacques Rousseau, a prestigious school in Saigon. The school was built in 1877 by the French and was originally called Collège Indigène. It was later renamed Collège Chasseloup Laubat after Marquis François de Chasseloup-Laubat. In 1954, the school was renamed Jean Jacques Rousseau with the intention of avoiding colonial reminiscent. However, it remained under the management of France's Department of Education. Many well-known people attended the historic school throughout the twentieth century. The list included French novelist Marguerite Duras, General Duong Van Minh, Historian Vuong Hong Sen, and Prince Norodom Sihanouk of Cambodia. In 1970, the school was transferred back to the government of the Republic of South Vietnam and was renamed Le Quy Don High School.

The school comprised four blocks of two-story buildings and occupied an entire block surrounded by four streets namely, Le Quy Don, Tran Quy Cap, Cong Ly, and Hong Thap Tu. Throughout the years, the school kept very much of its original structure. Across Le Quy Don street, there were many street vendors selling junk food to the students. One of the most popular foods was the papaya salad with beef jerky and hot sauce. It was so popular that often students had to wait for the kids in front of the line to finish eating first, so that the kids standing behind them could have their small aluminum plates quickly cleaned by the vendor, who would dip the plates into a dirty can of water hung by the side of his cart, and wipe them dry with a piece of cloth that looked like a dirty rag. But the students did not mind, as they always picked up the plates and drank all the hot sauce after they finished eating everything on the plates.

In the back of the school, across from Tran Quy Cap Street, there was a row of tall holly bushes behind a long iron black fence of a private villa that belonged to some French residents. One time when I arrived at school, I saw a group of boys climbing on top of each other to look behind the holly bushes. Curious, I left my bicycle at the curbside and jumped in to find out what was going on. I saw a naked French woman sun-bathing in the lounge chair in the backyard. All the boys, including myself, were captivated by the scene; it was something we could not find in any of our lessons in the classrooms. Vive la France!

We were obsessed with World War II movies, in which the Americans to us were always the good guys, the heroes who were out to save the world, and of course, the Nazis were always the bad guys. We all watched "The Longest Day" and knew by heart the French lyrics of the soundtrack "Le jour le plus long" from the movie. When "The Great Escape" under the French title "La Grande Évasion" came to Saigon, we cut classes to go see the movie. Most movies from Hollywood came to Saigon through France and, therefore, they all had French titles. It was one of the war movies with a huge all-star cast that included Steve McQueen, James Garner, Charles Bronson, and James Coburn, among others, and we could not miss it. We emptied our pockets to buy the tickets, locked our bicycles with a chain lock, and threw them on the ground in front of the Rex movie theater. We were lucky none of the bicycles were stolen before we came out of the theater because Saigon was known to be a haven for bicycle thieves.

We were also obsessed with graphic novels such as "Tintin et Milou," "Asterix," and "Lucky Luke," among others. We often exchanged the books with one another to read in class. There were days when classes ended early, and we would ride our bicycles to the Khai Tri bookstore to read books. The book store was located on Le Loi Blvd in the heart of Saigon. In the sixties, it was perhaps the only bookstore in Saigon where you could read books all day without having to buy anything. Another interesting thing about the bookstore was that back at that time, there was no security camera installed we knew of, but if someone walked out of the store with a book without paying, that person would certainly be stopped by the store employee. A boy in our group sneaked a Tintin book into his school bag. None of us knew about it until we walked toward the door, and an employee came out from nowhere, and stopped us and asked the boy to open his bag. We thought the store employee had to be mistaken because the boy did not need to steal any book - after all, his father was a well-known doctor and could buy him as many books as he wanted - but we were wrong. I guess kids will be kids; we all did stupid things when we were young.

The book store employee asked the boy to go with her to see the owner, whose office was on the second floor in the back of the store. The poor kid looked at us like he was about to cry. We did not know what to do, so we all hung around to wait for him. After a while, he came out and told us the owner just gave him a pep talk and let him go. Many years later, I learned that Mr. "Khai Tri"– as everyone called him since nobody really knew his name - did the same thing with a lot of kids who tried to steal books from his bookstore, as he never called the police or admonished them. Sometimes, he even gave the petty thief the book when he learned his parents were poor and could not afford to buy it for him. After the war ended, the communist government in Saigon launched the so-called "cultural re-education," they burned all the books in his store, and sent him to the re-education camp for selling "depraved" literature materials.

In high school, I started to hang out with the wrong crowd and was no longer the hardworking, rule-obeying, and diligent student I used to be. During a histoire/géographie class, I got into a problem with this French teacher. He was a rather old man in his sixties, overweight, and very difficult. He had a habit of throwing his old leather briefcase up in the air and catching it on the way down before sitting down in his chair. That morning, as usual, he walked into the classroom, threw his briefcase up, and shouted "L'Italie Primitive!"- "L'Italie Primitive" was the lesson of that day. Sitting in the front row, I mimicked his action by throwing my book up and catching it. The old man was not amused; he swung his pen out and gave me a "double 0" on the scorecard. As this was not enough, he also wrote "Taquiné le professeur," meaning "poking fun at the teacher," on my "*carnet de notes*" which my father would have to sign. Needless to say, my father almost ripped my head off when I showed him the note at the end of the month.

Another time in a French class, the teacher asked me what the definition of "nuance" is. I did not know the answer, so the teacher then asked if anyone else in the class knew what "nuance" meant. No one raised their hand. He asked again, and still total silence. He was so upset, he made the entire class write one hundred times on a piece of paper: *"La nuance, c'est une petite différence."* Even today, I still remember every single word of that definition.

Une petite différence was lost on a French official in a tale under the French colonial rule era, in which a French official asked a student what the name of the bridge across the Red River in Hanoi was. The Vietnamese student did not know the answer, so he got frustrated and blurted out "du me!"–a profanity for "mother fucker" in Vietnamese. To his surprise, the French official clapped his hand and congratulated him on the correct answer.

It turned out that the bridge was named after Paul Doumer, the Governor-General of French Indochina, whose last name is pronounced the same as "du me" in Vietnamese. The bridge was designed by Gustave Eiffel, the engineer who designed and built the Eiffel Tower in Paris, France. It was the first steel bridge in Hanoi, and at the time it was built, it was one of the four greatest bridges in the world. When Doumer returned to France from Indochina, he served as Minister of Finance and was later elected President of the French Republic in 1931. He was assassinated in 1932 by a mentally unstable Russian émigré. As for the bridge, it was later renamed to "Long

Bien" after the French left, and became a well-known landmark and target for U.S. pilots during the Vietnam War because of its important location connecting the two biggest cities in North Vietnam–Hanoi and Hai Phong. It was reported that despite many attempts at bombing it, the bridge was never directly hit, only partially damaged, and the communists were always quickly able to repair it. The bridge survived all the bombings and stood as a challenge to the supremacy of U.S. air power during the war.

During the sixties, smoking was widely popular in Saigon; everybody smoked. People smoked everywhere, outdoors, indoors, in coffee shops, movie theaters and even at schools. In particular, one of our teachers, Monsieur Hulot, who taught Français in quatrième, was a chain smoker. He always carried a cigarette pack in his shirt pocket. He came up with a creative way to call students up to recite their homework by choosing their names from the letters of the cigarette brand he was carrying. For example, if he was smoking SALEM that day, he would call the students whose first names begin with S, A, L, E and M. To keep us students guessing, he regularly changed the cigarette brand so we would not know what to expect. He really enjoyed tormenting us. As for him, it was a game that he took pleasure in playing. Monsieur Hulot also had a habit of pulling the students' ears when they did not do their homework. One time, he pulled the ear of a French kid named Jean-Marais so hard that his earlobe was ripped at the bottom. The next day his maman came to see Monsieur Hulot to complain and scold him to the extent that he had to apologize to her and the kid in front of the entire class.

In 1970, when Lycée Jean Jacques Rousseau was
returned to the Education Department of South Vietnam,
we were transferred to Lycée Marie Curie, which was a
prestigious all-girl high school in Saigon. There was a
surveillant there named Cảnh, who was a small fellow
with gray hair and probably in his forties. One thing that
stood out about Mr. Cảnh was that he always kept an
immaculate appearance, especially his black shoes, which
were always spotlessly shiny. The students called him
"Cảnh Hù." "Hù" means "bluff" thus "Cảnh Hù" means
"Cảnh who bluffs." Mr. Cảnh liked to write students up
for misbehaving while waiting in line to enter the
classrooms. However, the tickets he wrote carried no
weight, as they were more like a warning rather than
actual punishment, thus it earned him the nickname
"Cảnh Hù". The boys liked to pick on the poor man, and
they transposed his nickname from "Cảnh Hù" to "Củ
Hành" meaning "onion." Every time he walked by us, we
all shouted "Củ Hành" and he would get very agitated and
upset. He would threaten to send us to the *surveillant
général's* office, and we would immediately stop, which
gave him the impression that his threat worked. However,
as soon as he turned his back, the boys again would shout
"Củ Hành" and the cycle would start all over again.

Fast forward to half a century later, my cousin who
lives in Paris recently mentioned that about ten years ago
at a school reunion party in Paris, he met an old man who
introduced himself as "Cảnh Hù". He said the man was
very *"gentil"* and a true gentleman. Mr. Cảnh seemed to
be proud of his nickname; he talked about his memories,
the school, and the students. He said that memory may
fade over time, but his connection to the school was never

broken, and it was for that reason he went to the reunion to connect with the past he always cherished. Several years later, after the reunion, my cousin said he heard from Mr. Cảnh's son that he passed away peacefully in Paris.

At Marie Curie, I became a close friend with Khanh, a classmate. I usually went to his house to hang out and study together. One day he invited me to a New Year campfire, which the Saigon University Student Association organized. His sister was a member of the Association and said he could come along and invite a friend. I accepted wholeheartedly as I had never been to a campfire before. The event was held in the real estate of Long-Van Buddhist temple in Phu Lam district, about 8 miles from downtown Saigon. On the following Saturday morning, Khanh and I rode together on our bicycles and headed out to Phu Lam. It was a long trip on the bikes and when the sun came out above us; we were both sweating profusely. The Vietnamese New Year was around the corner, but Saigon was still hot and humid. We stopped by a vendor on the street side to get some cold lemonade for refreshment before continuing on. When we finally got to Phu Lam, we saw a dirt road off the main road on the left, with many "Land for Sale" signs popping up near the intersection.

"The temple should be at the end of the dirt road." Khanh said.

We followed the long dirt road and soon we saw the curved roof of the temple appearing from afar. As we came upon the end of the road, Long Van temple emerged as a lone building in the middle of nowhere. The subtle smell of incense from inside the temple gave us a sense of tranquility; suddenly we felt at peace as if we just entered a different world. It was quite a contrast to the noisy main road that we just came from.

As we entered the temple, I saw a young woman talking to an old monk in the main hall. I took a wild guess that she must be Khanh's sister. Before I could ask, Khanh already confirmed my suspicion that she was indeed his sister. Her name was Phuong, and she was rather pretty with her long black hair. She wore the white traditional Vietnamese "*áo dài*" which was a staple of uniform for all school girls in Saigon.

It seemed we were early as not too many people had arrived yet; Phuong told us we could walk around seeing the estate. I noticed the temple was still under construction since besides the main hall, other parts of the building had not been completed. While we were walking around, I took the opportunity to ask Khanh about his sister; he said Phuong was a junior at the Saigon University and a member of the student association. She had been actively involved in social activities to help raise money for the construction of Long Van temple.

While we were outside, people began to arrive, and the place seemed more vibrant with different activities. When the sun had set at the end of the horizon, we all gathered in the courtyard in front of the temple, forming a large circle. One person started the fire at the center of the courtyard and two others carried out a large pot and set it up over the fire. They then loaded it with dozens of square cakes of rice and pork wrapped with green banana leaves called "*banh chung*". Khanh and I were tasked with watching the fire and to add water to the pot to cook the "*banh chung*." Soon, everyone had gathered around the fire and was singing popular Vietnamese folk songs. As the night progressed, the songs became more political with anti-war tones. I watched Phuong from across the firelight and saw her face was blushing from the warm heat of the fire. I could see it in her eyes that she was a passionate person, the type of person who would devote herself to the cause she believed in, whether wrongly or rightly.

It was a starry night and as the temperature got colder, everyone was getting closer to the fire and to each other to keep warm. The sounds of the guitar strumming and the voices singing filled the air of the quiet night. From the direction of the temple appeared two silhouettes, and as they came closer, I recognized the old monk and a new, younger figure we had not seen all night. The old monk introduced the young man to the group as Manh and said that he had just been released from prison because of his anti-government and anti-war activities. Everyone applauded as the old monk finished his introduction. Phuong came over to greet him; it appeared that they knew each other. It was then that I realized the group of young university students I had been with all night was part of an anti-war organization disguised as a student association, and many were probably Viet Cong (VC) sympathizers. Although I was too young to know at the time, I felt something was not right. People like Phuong and her friends were too naïve and perhaps exploited by men like Manh. I had also always wondered about the role of the Buddhist organizations in supporting anti-war and anti-government movements while claiming freedom of religion. Their actions had caused severe damage to the stability of the South Vietnam Government in its effort to fight the communist insurgents.

During the spring of 1972, the North Vietnamese Communists again launched major attacks against South Vietnam (SVN). As the war had intensified, the government lowered the draft age from eighteen to seventeen in order to meet the demand of the battlefields. By 1972, I had left French school and enrolled in a Vietnamese high school and barely avoided the draft; about half of the boys in my class received the draft papers and had to drop out of school to join the military. By this time, the number of U.S. troops in Vietnam had been reduced from a peak of 549,000 in 1969 to 69,000, mostly in support roles as a result of Nixon's Vietnamization policy. The Vietnamization policy, in a nutshell, was a strategy to transfer the combat responsibility from the U.S. to South Vietnam.

The communists wanted to test the effectiveness of the Vietnamization strategy and believed that they could easily overwhelm the Army of the Republic of South Vietnam (ARVN) based on their previous victory in Laos. Unlike the Tet Offensive in 1968, this time the communists were well prepared with modern warfare equipment, and for the first time in the history of the Vietnam War, they conducted a conventional invasion using regular infantry of the People's Army of Vietnam (PAVN) with armor assaults backed by heavy artillery. Prior to the offensive, the PAVN had received specialized training and a flood of equipment and supplies for a modern conventional army from China and the Soviet. The equipment included Soviet made T-34 & T-54 tanks, Chinese made T-59s, PT-76 light amphibious tanks, hundreds of anti-aircraft missiles and long-range artillery. The PAVN deployed 14 divisions to attack across the four military zones of South Vietnam.

After initial setbacks, the ARVN fought back with relentless U.S. air support and recaptured most territories taken by the communists. The PAVN had to halt their offensive after they suffered heavy and irreplaceable losses. The human costs on both sides were huge, but the North Vietnamese leadership had underestimated the fighting ability of ARVN and the supreme air power support from the U.S.

After the U.S. combat forces left in 1973, the ARVN was left to fight the communists all by itself with limited supplies and no U.S. air support, while the North Vietnamese communists received unlimited support from their two patrons, China and the Soviet Union. It pains me that all conventional history books, including history channels, have all portrayed the ARVN in such unfair and demeaning manners. This characterization even dates back to the early period before the U.S. combat troops were directly involved in the war. The ARVN was often criticized for poor performance by the U.S. media, which relied heavily on information from young and naïve journalists, such as David Halberstam, Neil Sheehan, and Stanley Karnow. According to author and historian Mark Moyar, "Sheehan and Halberstam came to Vietnam believing they were entitled to receive all the information they wanted, and when government officials did not follow their script, the two young men became indignant and vengeful."

The two young reporters supported the American involvement in Vietnam, but they despised president Ngo Dinh Diem and decided themselves that in order for the war to be won, Diem would need to be removed. Like other foreign journalists in Saigon, Halberstam and Sheehan received their information from a man named Phạm Xuân Ẩn who worked for Reuters and then, Time Magazine. Ẩn was highly regarded as "a trusted source of information". He usually spent his days at a Givral Café, a popular place in Saigon where local and foreign correspondences hung out to hunt for information on the war, but most of the information Ẩn shared was false and misleading. [8]

After the fall of Saigon in 1975, it was revealed that Ẩn was a top Viet Cong spy and a lieutenant colonel in the Liberation Army. In the autobiography book "Perfect Spy," Larry Berman wrote that "Ẩn was the most valuable of all agents operating in the South, precisely because he had already established an almost impenetrable cover." His early reports were so accurate that General Vo Nguyen Giap, the key architect of the Dien Bien Phu battle against the French, joked, "We are now in the U.S.'s war room."

Ẩn described the time that he was in California and went to college in Costa Mesa as the best time of his life and said that he loved America. He also stated that he was a patriot, and that everything he did was for his country. He told Stanley Karnow that his love for Vietnam had not diminished his love for America. To be clear, this was the man who, during the Tet Offensive in 1968, was part of the team who planned the tactics for the operation to kill

Vietnamese people and Americans. Before the attack, he drove the Viet Cong commander, General Tran Van Tra, around Saigon to show him the infiltration routes and the best targets in his old Renault French-made car. Many Vietnamese and Americans, including innocent people, died because of his clandestine activities. When the North Vietnamese Army entered Saigon and ended the war in 1975, he sent his wife and four children to the U.S. through his connection with Time Magazine, although he was forced to call them back home later by the communist ruler.

Was he a hero, or was he just a hypocrite and an opportunist who played on both sides? Surprisingly, some of his former American colleagues still felt for him and considered him an American hero because one time, he saved one of his colleagues, an American journalist, from the Viet Cong during the war. From my perspective, Ẩn was neither an American hero nor a Vietnamese hero. He had betrayed his friends and his own people, and I hope one day, history will judge him accordingly.

According to Moyar, "Halberstam, Sheehan, and Karnow inadvertently caused enormous damage to the American effort in South Vietnam–making them the most harmful journalists in American history." Halberstam's journalism career started in Mississippi where he covered the Civil Rights Movement, and when he came to Vietnam, he expected South Vietnam, a country at war, to possess levels of political virtues that even in the U.S. were not always applied. For example, he wrote about his perception of how brothers Diem and Nhu suppressed Buddhism, and how the secret police had cracked down on people who demonstrated against the government. He then compared the situation in Saigon with that in Hanoi, which he stated had no demonstrations there. Perhaps Halberstam forgot North Vietnam was a communist and police state, where anti-government demonstrations were not allowed, and people would be charged with anti-revolutionary crime and jailed or shot if they protested.

When the new U.S. Ambassador to Vietnam, Henry Cabot Lodge, first arrived in Saigon, the people he met first to find out about the situation in Vietnam were not U.S. and Vietnam government officials, but Halberstam and Sheehan. Lodge believed the information he received from the two American journalists over the official reports from the CIA and the U.S. military. Based on the information from Halberstam and Sheehan, Lodge intentionally circumvented president Kennedy and urged the South Vietnamese generals to stage the coup.

I could say that the appointment of Henry Cabot Lodge as U.S. Ambassador sealed the fate of President Diem. President Kennedy had worried about Lodge, a Republican Senator from Massachusetts, who could run against him in the next presidential election in 1964, so he sent Lodge away to Vietnam. The appointment of Lodge was a mistake, just like the removal of President Diem was a mistake. Ironically, three weeks after Diem and his brother Nhu were murdered, President Kennedy was assassinated on November 22, 1963, in Dallas, Texas. No one knows exactly how the Vietnam War would have ended if President Diem had not been removed and murdered, but one thing is certain: Because Diem was adamant about not having U.S. combat troops in Vietnam, were he still in power, tens of thousands U.S. lives could have been saved.

The Vietnam War was not just a civil war between the North and the South, but an ideology of warfare between the free world and communism. The U.S. chose South Vietnam as the place to stop the spread of communism after it failed to do so in Laos, as per the domino theory. South Vietnam was then given a fancy name as "The Anti-Communist Outpost of the Free World." Moyar pointed out that under President Diem, South Vietnam actually did achieve much progress on the battlefield against the communist insurgents and that Diem's Strategic Hamlet program was a success in the pacification effort of the countryside. Diem believed that with continued U.S. military aid, his army would be capable of fighting the war on its own. He was against the idea of bringing U.S. combat troops to Vietnam for the fear of losing its principle that Vietnam was not an independent state, and falling into the communist propaganda trap that his presidency and his army were just America's puppet. He was right. A little more than a year after his death, the U.S. Marines landed on the beach of Da Nang and marked the beginning of the U.S. active involvement in and the Americanization of the war.

The application of the domino theory to contain the spread of communism in Southeast Asia was a noble idea, but the policy of containment to support it was doomed from the beginning, at least with the Vietnam War. By implementing the policy of containment, the U.S. basically was not looking for victory, but rather, it only played defense. The U.S. military was not allowed to cross the 17th parallel to attack North Vietnam for the fear it would draw the Chinese into the conflict. It was like in football; you started your offense at the twenty-yard line, and you moved the ball to mid-field then you could not cross it. Meanwhile, your opponent could freely attack you across mid-field. It made no sense.

Like most young men of my age, the senior year in high school was the most important - a "do or die" situation for us. The military draft system required all young men of age eighteen to pass the national exam with a Baccalaureate Certificate in order to be eligible for the educational deferment. That year, I went to a private Vietnamese school in downtown Saigon. The school used to be a hotel and was converted to a high school for seniors. It was in the heart of Saigon, and across the street was the dental office of Dr. Bui Dinh Can, father of my friend Bui Quoc Lan from Lycée Marie Curie.

Right on the first day of class, I noticed a pretty girl sitting across from me; she was always looking at me with sparkling eyes and then she would look away when I looked back at her. She had a special way to smile with her eyes without actually smiling, which attracted my attention. I offered to give her a ride home after school on my Yamaha motorbike and learned that her name was K.H. Soon I would give her a ride home every day, and we often stopped by the street vendor stands to eat and hang out. She also came to visit me sometimes during the weekend. One time while I was up on the plum tree to pick the big red plums for my grandmother, she came by unexpectedly and caught me off guard since I was wearing only my shorts. It was hot that day, and I could see the twinkle in her eyes with that little grin on her face like the first time I saw her.

One beautiful Saturday, my friend Cung and I went

with K.H. and her friend to visit Hiep, a friend who was going through basic training at the Thu Duc Infantry Academy, about 20 miles outside of Saigon. The four of us on two motorbikes headed out onto Highway One after crawling through the city traffic. It was a perfect morning, with the open road in front of us; I felt the thrill and excitement as I shifted to higher gear and twisted down hard on the throttle to speed up. The Yamaha hesitated, then jumped forward, making a roaring noise as it accelerated. The wind was blowing around us and I could feel K.H. wrapping her arms around my waist tighter and her hair was blowing wildly. About an hour later, we arrived in front of the school. At the entrance gate, we saw a big sign that read:

"Thao trường đổ mồ hôi, chiến trường bớt đổ máu," which is literally the Navy SEAL maxim:

"The more you sweat in training, the less you bleed in battle."

The Thu Duc Infantry School was one of the five training schools for officers of the ARVN. The other four are Da Lat Military Academy, Da Lat Political Warfare University, Nha Trang Airforce Academy, and Nha Trang Naval Academy. It was established in 1951 by the decree signed by Head of State Bao Dai, and the first class was opened on October 9, 1951. From 1951 to 1975, the school had trained over 99,000 officers of the ARVN. During the last few months of the war, my aunt's husband, colonel Tran Duc M., was the last commander of the school. He oversaw the defense of the school against the attack of North Vietnamese forces, in which the South Vietnamese military cadets destroyed a North Vietnamese T-54 tank before surrendering on April 30, knew who the culprits were. He said this was a warning, and that if it happened again, the students would be expelled from school. Although I was not involved, hearing my name called out in front of the entire class was pretty embarrassing. As he finished speaking, we heard loud boos throughout the room. Feeling that his authority was being challenged, the man said that he was an ex-secret police officer and would welcome anyone who wanted to challenge him. As he was speaking, he tapped the belt under his shirt, pretending as if there was a gun or weapon there. More loud boos erupted. I whispered to Hải, "This guy is a clown!"

It seemed as if misfortune kept following me. One day, I had an afternoon class, so I went to the coffee place in the morning to meet with a friend before heading to school. While I was sitting at our table, a kid wearing a blue uniform from the Cao Thang polytechnic school came over. Apparently, he overheard us talking and learned that I was a student at Van Hoa High, so he came over to make trouble. I learned through him that there was a feud between the two schools, and that about a year ago, the Cao Thang students came to Van Hoa and attacked the students there. The school had to be closed for several days because the students were afraid to go back to school. The police got involved to guarantee the safety of the students in order for the school to be reopened. This kid warned me they will come again to look for a fight around the Moon Festival holiday. I realized we were outnumbered, the two of us against about six of them, so we just stood up and left. At school, I told Hải what happened at the coffee place. We never discussed it again, and I had forgotten all about it.

Unbeknown to us, a kid sitting behind us overheard our conversation. He told his friends about what he heard and he decided to call up students to prepare for an anticipated battle with the other school. Soon the rumor spread all over the school, however, I knew nothing about it until one morning, Hai asked me,

"Did you see the notice from the Security Office?"

"What notice?"

"The notice that was posted everywhere in front of each classroom."

I went to our classroom and saw the notice affixed to the door. As I read it, I could feel my back sweating. It read:

"Recently someone has spread a false rumor intending to exploit and create conflict between our school and Cao Thang school. This person has called up students to prepare for an upcoming attack from the students at Cao Thang during the Moon Festival holiday. If you know or have any information about who that person is, you are to let the head of security know immediately, so proper actions can be taken. The school has notified the Saigon Police Department. We want you to know the safety of our students is our number one priority."

Millions of questions raced through my mind: "What the heck is going on?" "Where did this come from?" "I said nothing like that to anyone. How did the head of security know about this?"

I wondered if Hai spread the rumor, but I knew he would not do something like that. It made me so nervous when I sat in the classroom, I could not focus on anything the teacher said. I felt like I was sitting on a time bomb the tank of my Yamaha to make sure it had plenty of gas. I prayed my motorbike would run smoothly as it had occasionally died on me during the most unfortunate moment–like the first time I took K.H. home after school. On the way to the testing center, I saw a friend who was waving at me as he passed by me in his father's Jeep, which was driven by a chauffeur in military uniform. I murmured, "Lucky guy!"

The first day went smoothly, as I felt I did well with the test. After I went home, I continued to prepare for day two. There was no quitting now, as I was so close to the finishing line. Another sleepless night and it would be all over. The second day did not go as well as the first one since I had struggled with some subjects, one of which was math. Skipping math class early in the year was not a good idea after all, as it had come back to bite me during the test.

When the results were available about a month later, I went to the test center to check. A crowd already gathered at the bulletin board in front of the center. Fighting the crowd to get closer to the bulletin board where the results were posted, I tried desperately to look for my name. When I finally found my name on the list, I heaved an enormous sigh of relief and was so happy that tears were running down my face. I looked around and saw many happy as well as sad faces. I saw a friend who did not make the list, and he proclaimed in despair:

"The government had conspired to suppress talents in order to fulfill the demand of the battlefield!"

I passed the exam with a B minus average, which is nothing to be proud of, but considering that I did it without the help of any teachers, I thought it was worth a celebration. Weeks later, we threw a graduation ball party and invited K.H. and all of our friends to celebrate.

After we graduated from high school, K.H. and I went on to different universities, and somehow, we just drifted apart, as we did not see each other as often as we used to. The last time I saw her was when we ran into each other on the street in Saigon; we stopped and chatted for a while. Then, when the war ended, I left Vietnam, and I never saw her again.

BROWN ANGEL

In 1954, my grandparents bought a house in the district of Phu-Nhuan in a residential area called Chu Manh Trinh. My parents also had a house built not too far from my grandparents. It was the house that we grew up in, but I also spent a lot of time at my grandparents' place. My brother Thang and I often visited our grandparents and played with their dog in the big yard and sometimes we slept over. My grandparents had a talking Mynah bird, but the only thing it could say was "có khách, có khách" which meant "have visitor, have visitor." Indeed, the bird was never wrong, as whenever there was a visitor, it would always announce this on the spot. I remember a man who used to come to visit my grandfather, and the bird would always say "có khách, có khách," never missing a beat. He was a tall man with a head full of white hair, and his name was Dr. Thìn. He did not visit my grandfather to make house calls, but to smoke opium with him.

Opium was illegal in the South, but its use can be traced back to the post-colonial Vietnam. During the first Indochina War (1946- 54), French and Viet Minh actors actively pursued the opium production and trade in the Black River region near the borders of China and Laos. [9] In the first half of the twentieth century, opium monopoly functioned as a significant revenue for the colonial government in which it handled the operation of manufacturing, and production of opium in the entire region. Although nationalist leaders condemned the monopoly, opium revenue likewise helped the Viet Minh Front and the early Democratic Republic of Vietnam (DRV) build an army and finance its government. [10]After defeating France at the Battle of Dien Bien Phu and during the Second Indochina War (1965-75) [11], the DRV exerted monopoly control over the vast region's opium production and distribution, including heroin production in the Golden Triangle, a region where the borders of Thailand, Laos and Myanmar meet.

When U.S. troops arrived in Vietnam later during the war, the U.S. military used opium as a practice to combat guerilla forces. This practice was very common among the troops when the U.S. gained control of the Philippines in 1898. [12] The drug used in the U.S. Army was not limited to opium, but it also included alcohol, marijuana, amphetamine, and heroin. According to a report in 1971; 28% of U.S. soldiers fighting in the Vietnam War were heroin addicts. [13] Many reasons contributed to the widespread addiction: heroin was cheap, easy to purchase in Vietnam, and in part because of the breakdown in morale in the Army.

As a member of the coalition government, and later

as a mayor of Hanoi, my grandfather probably had access to opium and picked up the habit when he was still in North Vietnam. The use of opium in the South was prohibited and addiction was not as prevalent as in the North, but people like my grandfather, who could afford it, could get it through their informal connections. I always suspected Dr. Thìn was the source because my grandfather only smoke opium with him, and it was quite possible that Dr. Thìn brought it with him every time he came to see my grandfather.

Dr. Thìn usually came after dinner to enjoy a few doses with my grandfather. They wanted me to hang out by the "divan," which is a flat wooden bed where they laid facing each other with the opium tray in between them so they could share the equipment and the opium. All I could remember as a ten-year-old boy at the time was that it took a long time for them to prepare for one dose. I usually just stood there and watched my grandfather use a long needle with a pea-sized ball of the black opium paste at one end and hold it over the flame of the lamp, which is called the "spirit lamp." He would hold it until the opium bubble swelled and became soft and sticky. He would then keep stretching it into a long string then roll it back into the pea shape, as if he were cooking it, and do the same thing repeatedly until finally he would push the opium into the hollow in the bowl of the long wooden pipe. With the bowl close to the flame, he would take a deep pull at the pipe, making a noise like fine crackles sound. He would repeat this a few times until the opium was completely consumed. After each pull, he would exhale and release a wave of smoke. I could smell the fragrance of the opium as it was going up to the ceiling. The opium smoke was so powerful and addictive even to the house geckos; they all came out to inhale it, and sometimes they were so intoxicated they dropped from the ceiling to the floor. When both my grandfather and Dr. Thìn finished, they would lie on their back with their eyes closed as they enjoyed the opium ecstasy. It is no wonder it is called the "joy plant" in South East Asia, and the "brown angel" in Vietnam.

It was at that moment when they would finish smoking that I would serve them hot tea and peanut candy bars. That was my job and, as a reward, my grandfather would tell me his favorite ghost stories. That was the best part of the night I would have waited patiently for. The following are some of the ghost stories that my grandfather told me.

* * *

The Three Students

It was said a long time ago in a village in North Vietnam, there were three students who were studying for their upcoming exam. They studied into the night, but suddenly one of them felt ill and died. Since they were in a remote village, and it was pretty late, they lay their dead friend on the table in the middle of the room and cover him with a bed sheet. They planned to watch him and wait until morning to notify the authorities.

As the night progressed, they got bored, since there

was not much for them to do. They could not focus on their study anyway, so one student suggested he would go out to see if he could find something to eat. After his friend left, the third student waited for a while, then he thought of playing a prank on his friend. He stood his dead friend behind the front door, then he laid on the table and covered himself with the bedsheet. When the other student returned, he slowly rose to scare his friend. The other student thought it was his dead friend who came back from the death, so he dashed to the door and ran. The wicked student did not want his prank to stop, so he chased after him. As he passed through the front door and ran after his friend, he suddenly heard footsteps running behind him. He turned his head around and saw his dead friend. Terrified, he tried to run faster, but in doing so, his friend in front of him got more frightened and ran even faster. In the night's darkness, three shadows kept running and no one could stop.

The next morning, people in the village discovered three bodies laid on top of each other. The body on top was cold, but the two bodies underneath were still warm. After preliminary investigation, they determined that the student with the cold body had been probably dead for a while but somehow was attracted to the other two students by static electricity. They hypothesized that when the two students ran past by the dead body, their motions created the static electricity strong enough to make the body attracted to them and ran after them.

* * *

Corner Ghost

During the French colonial time, the French liked to hunt tiger in the highland areas of Northern Vietnam. This is the mountainous region where the inhabitants comprised the Hmong (Mèo), Thai, Khmu (Xá), Lao, Dao (Mien), and others whom the Vietnamese called in general the "Thượng" or highland people.

According to legend, one day, a French officer went hunting with a group of Vietnamese in the highland area. After a day of hunting, the group came to a stilt house owned by a Thượng family. They went inside to rest and look for something to eat, as they were all tired and hungry after a long day of hunting.

The Thượng people were well known to be very hospitable, in which their door was always open and guests were always welcome to their house, even if they were not home. It so happened that on that day, the entire family was out, so the group went inside and found some dry pork and sticky rice wrapped in banana leaves on the nearby table. They helped themselves to the food. The Thượng used little furniture and there were no chairs in the tiny hut, so everyone sat on the floor to rest. The French officer was not used to sitting on the floor; he looked around to find anything that he could sit on. He saw a long wooden box standing in a corner of the room, so he took it down and sat on it. After a while, the group left after leaving a nice sum of money for the Thượng family.

When the group got back to town, the Frenchman felt ill and, several days later, he could not move. Doctors had given up, as they did not know what was wrong with him. As he was laying in his bed waiting for his death, he recalled his hunting trip and the visit to the house of the Thượng. A knowledgeable Vietnamese asked him if he had come upon a wooden box in the house and if he had sat on it. The Frenchman said yes. The Viet explained to him it is a custom of the Thượng to keep the dead inside a wooden box at home to guard their house. When the French officer sat on the box, he violated the spirit and was probably being punished for his actions. The Viet recommended he set up an altar with proper rituals, bow and pray to the god and the spirit of the dead to ask for forgiveness. The French officer obliged and several days later, he completely recovered.

The worst part was that after listening to these ghost stories, I had to walk home alone on the dark road, and although it was only about a fifteen-minute walk, it would feel like an eternity. One time, late at night, the small road was pretty dark, and the light of the crescent moon above me was barely visible. Sucking up all the courage I had and telling myself that there was nothing to be afraid of, I held my breath and walked fast. As I passed by a big willow tree, where I had heard a rumor that a woman had hung herself there, I felt goosebumps all over my body. I ran as fast as I could. As I ran, I felt a cold air on the back of my neck, as if someone was chasing me and breathing down on it. When I finally got home, I was still shaking. While I had not completely caught my breath, my mother saw me and she said:

"You look like you were just chased by a ghost or something!"

THE WOODEN CHEST

After moving to the South, my grandfather worked for several private companies, then retired. He later came out of retirement to work for his friend Hoang Kim Quy, an entrepreneur and businessman whom he knew from Hanoi. During that time, he studied English and eventually became chairperson of the Vietnam British Association and received an honorary medal as an officer of the Order of the British Empire (OBE). He is probably the only Vietnamese citizen who has ever received an OBE. He then worked for the U.S. Embassy with Dr. Douglas Pike.

In 1966, he was invited to a reception for all OBE recipients in London, hosted by Queen Elizabeth. The U.S. Government funded his trip with the condition that he would speak on the British and Belgian radio programs about the war in Vietnam. After he returned from overseas, his friend Hoang Kim Quy invited my grandfather to join him on his ticket to run for the Senate

45

of the Republic of South Vietnam. After he won the election, he was selected as chairman of the Senate Foreign Relations Committee and was a leading and vocal political opponent of the president and his administration. He was the deputy chief of the major opposition bloc in the senate. As such, he was often regarded by some Americans as the Senator Fulbright of South Vietnam, but unlike Fulbright, he strongly supported the U.S. involvement in the war against the Hanoi communist government. He also served as vice president of South Vietnam's Anti-Communist League. Given his personal experience, he opposed a coalition government and firmly believed that the communists would never agree to any peaceful resolution to end the war.

Because of his position, my grandfather received a lot of gifts from many people, including many foreign dignitaries. However, he was an honorable man and only accepted small gifts here and there, such as bottles of wine and liquor, and never anything of high cash value. Nevertheless, he soon found himself owning a lot of bottles of all different types and brands, and he did not know what to do with them since he was not a drinker. He needed to find a place to store these bottles, and then he discovered that underneath the bottom drawer of the wooden chest he kept in his bedroom, there was a space that was large enough to store the bottles. It was an old and beautiful wooden chest made of solid oak wood, which must have been custom crafted with a serpentine design and dovetailed drawers. It could have been imported from France for all I knew, as my grandparents probably had it in Hanoi and brought it with them when they moved to the South. The chest had some minor signs of wear and use, but it looked like a beautiful, classic chest with three drawers. My grandparents kept all kinds of miscellaneous items in the drawers, from silverware and china sets to old picture albums, among other items. My grandfather asked me to help him load the bottles into the secret compartment of the wooden chest. He told me it was a secret between him and me, and that even my grandmother would not know. At the time, I did not think much about our little secret, and I had forgotten all about it as I grew older.

In 1972, while my grandfather was preparing to travel to the U.S. for a meeting, he felt ill and was admitted to the Grall Hospital in Saigon. I went to see him with my father and he appeared to be in good spirits, but his health took a turn for the worse several days after our visit. The doctors explained his lungs suffered severe damage, probably because of years of smoking opium and that there was nothing they could do for him. My grandmother decided to bring him home so that he could be with his family. The next day, I stayed up all night by his bed, but he never woke up and I watched him pass peacefully that night.

The office of the South Vietnam President sent an army officer to assist with logistic issues regarding the funeral arrangement. There were many public figures from congress and the government and foreign dignitaries who came to pay their final respects. After the funeral, my grandparents' house seemed bigger and emptier, and my grandmother spent most of her time going to her friends to play mahjong. I stopped coming over as often as I used to and completely forgot about the wooden chest and the bottles.

In my senior year in high school, I started to hang out at the café places with a group of friends after school. It had become a trend for young people in Saigon to go to the café places to drink coffee, chat, smoke, talk about girls, the war, and the future, and sometimes just to hang out. We were learning to be adults and wanted to appear serious and intellectual, so we carried books such as Leo Tolstoy's "War and Peace" and Dostoyevsky's "The Brothers Karamazov", but in reality, we only read a few chapters and never finished reading those thick and boring books we borrowed from the national library. Since the allowance from our parents was not enough to pay for the leisure to drink and smoke regularly at the café places, we had to sell our old clothes and other personal items at the open market to get extra cash.

A woman at the open market asked if I had any wine or liquor bottles to sell. She said that wine and liquor were easier to sell, and that she would pay good money to buy them. Suddenly, a light bulb went off in my head as I remembered the wooden chest and the bottles that were hidden underneath the bottom drawer. I was not sure if the bottles were still there, as it had been nearly a decade since I helped my grandfather to load the bottles there. I decided I would go back to my grandmother's place to check it out.

The opportunity came when my grandmother, as usual, went out to play mahjong - I went to the wooden chest and removed the last drawer. And there they were, stacking neatly in rows on top of each other and covered with a thin layer of dust throughout the years. I felt like a thief who had just discovered a treasure. I took one bottle out and quickly replaced the drawer. My heart was beating fast, as if I were about to be caught of committing a major crime. I took the bottle and rushed to the open market to sell it to the woman.

"Young man," the woman said.

"No one would buy this bottle. It looks like a fish sauce bottle; there is no brand name, and the top looks like it was already opened."

She then showed me a bottle of Cognac and told me to bring something similar. This was my first lesson that I learned about wine and liquor. It turned out that in my moment of haste; I had grabbed my grandfather's medicinal liquor, because I thought that the older the bottle looked, the more valuable it would be, and did not realize that the bottle did not have any label or brand name. The first time is always the hardest, but I learned quickly, with the help of the woman at the open market, about the many types of wine and liquor that buyers would want to buy. Then one by one, I brought to her bottles of Hennessy, Cognac, Napoleon, Martell, and Courvoisier; then came Johnny Walker, Jack Daniel and different brands of wine.

With the extra cash from selling the wine and liquor bottles, I became a regular customer at some of the most popular café places in Saigon. These places not only served coffee but they also always played the most recent top music hits from the U.S., as well as French hits, from famous bands and artists such as The Beatles, The Rolling Stones, CCR, The BeeGees, The Carpenters, Joe Dassin, Salvatore Adamo, Art Sullivan, Francois Hardy, Sylvie Vartan, Christophe, and Charles Aznavour, among others.

Many years after I left Saigon and came to the U.S., I learned that after my grandmother passed away, my uncle sold the house to a communist cadre. The communist is probably now the new owner of the wooden chest, but he will never know that underneath the bottom of the chest was once a secret treasure and a part of my childhood memory that I will never forget.

THE STREET VENDOR

Nobody knew where he came from or what his actual name was, but everyone would call him "Cụ Lý". "Cụ" is a title given to people who are old, usually over seventy years, and "Lý" is just a common last name. Used together, 'Cụ Lý' is not a real name, but is more like the fictional character "Lý Toét" from Northern Vietnam, whose name is often used to describe someone who is moronic.

Although he was called "Cụ Lý", he was actually only in his early or mid-40s, and was average looking with a medium build. He always combed his hair back in the classic slicked back hairstyle, using brilliantines or an oil-based pomade to keep it in place. All year round, he only wore a short-sleeved white shirt that had turned into an off-white color and a pair of dark navy-blue pants. For footwear, he wore a pair of sandals that he called "Nam-Dinh sandals," but nobody knew exactly what they were or if they were really from Nam-Dinh; a region in the Red

River Delta of North Vietnam. His accent was certainly from the North, and it could have even been the Nam-Dinh accent, but who knew? If people did not pay close attention, they could have mistaken him for a government worker because of the way he dressed; white shirt and blue navy pants were typical attire for people who worked for the government at the time.

The origin of his nickname may have also derived from the fact that his eyes were always red and watery like those of the fictional character "Lý Toét." In reality, he probably suffered from a medical condition called conjunctivitis or pinkeye. Notwithstanding, he liked the nickname perhaps because he did not have to reveal his real name or true identity. Rumor had it that the man actually existed before 1954 in Hanoi. According to Song Thao, a Vietnamese writer who lives in Canada, Cụ Lý used to sell French bread in front of the Dzung-Lac high school in Hanoi but the students there called him "Lý Toét," the same name as the aforementioned fictional character. It appeared that he only adopted the name "Cụ Lý" after he migrated to the South at the end of the first Indochina War.

Every morning, people saw Cụ Lý riding a blue Mobylette to a villa in a quiet alley off Hai Ba Trung Street. Upon arriving at the big iron gate, he would put his hand through a hole in the gate to open it from the inside. He would perform the task meticulously, as he had done it so many times before. Inside the courtyard, at a corner, was a three-wheel food cart. He would park his Mobylette next to it and unload the fresh hot rolls of French baguettes and dozens of Vietnamese pork sausage tightly wrapped in banana leaves from the basket in the back of

his Mobylette onto the food cart. Carefully, he would
push the food cart out to the alley and park it under the
villa's long wall covered with purple flowers. Nobody
knew what his relationship with the villa owner was;
however, people just knew that the owner was a history
teacher at Lycée Marie Curie and that Cụ Lý probably
rented the little corner of the courtyard to store his food
cart there. Around 7:00 am, a line would slowly form at
the food cart to buy Cụ Lý's famous baguettes called
"bánh mì" and Vietnamese pork sausage. It was
customary to see the long line extend all the way out to
Hai Ba Trung Street.

The history of "bánh mì" is that the French bread
originally followed the footsteps of the French
expeditionary soldiers to Indochina in the early 19th
century, and was made there locally to feed the hungry
soldiers. During the colonization of Indochina, French
bread then become a part of Vietnamese food and
culture. In Vietnam, French bread became "bánh mì" and
the Vietnamese people transformed it into a delicatessen
by adding various ingredients, but it still carried some
French taste.

Bánh mì Cụ Lý, on the other hand, had been totally
Vietnamized - and I am not referring to the war here,
mind you. His bánh mì was in fact pretty simple; the
bread was cut into palm size pieces and filled with
Vietnamese pork sausage and thin slices of fresh onion.
Then he would lightly spray them with diluted fish sauce
mixed with vinegar and chopped garlic. That's it! No
mayonnaise, no butter, no Maggi, no other added

ingredients, but somehow people were addicted to it. When you ate it once, you would want to eat it again and again. If you missed it for one day, you would feel like your day was not complete. It was like a smoker missing his cigarette after a meal.

His customers were usually young male high school students, but there were also some university students and government workers. Some folks drove their automobiles into the alley to buy his bánh mì and he would get very upset and refuse to sell to them, even when they offered to pay three or four times the regular price. By noon, he would sell out all of his bánh mì and sausage, and would only keep some to sell to his special and regular customers. This was when he would open up and tell you stories about his life, but most, if not all, were made up to make you laugh. The students did not care though, as we really enjoyed his stories and the hilarious laughs. Sometimes we laughed so hard, tears would come to our eyes. He was an excellent storyteller, and very articulate.

Cụ Lý considered my friends and I his regular customers, and we would always come in the afternoon to buy his bánh mì and listen to his stories. He said he made a lot of money selling bánh mì, but then he would use all of his money to buy lottery tickets and never win anything. He also said he was married to a "Tokyo madame" who lived in another country, so he would have to fly on a "Caravelle" airplane every time he wanted to visit her. We all knew that these were made up stories, but none of us seemed to mind.

His customers were usually young male students, for whom he would always wrap their bánh mì with pages of nude pictures from old Playboy magazines that he bought from the open market and stored carefully on the bottom shelf of his food cart. This was probably why many people suspected that Cụ Lý was a sexual predator who preyed on young boys, but some people also believed that he was a Viet Cong agent who tried to recruit young students. No one knew for sure the mystery surrounding the man and his secrecy, but one thing everyone agreed upon was that his bánh mì was undoubtedly famous and popular among all the students during those years.

After the war, he continued to sell bánh mì in Saigon. It had become popular not only among students but also in the working class. In 1996, the Tuoi Tre Magazine listed "Bánh Mì Cụ Lý" in a book of 100 best fast-food places in Saigon. He later retired in 2003 and turned over the business to his nephew. It was said that after he retired, he returned to North Vietnam and died of old age there. He was never married.

NOSTALGIA: FOREVER SAIGON

Saigon was once called "Pearl of the Far East" by the French during its colonial period, perhaps because they had invested heavily in Saigon and had planned for it to become the capital of Indochina, or perhaps they wanted it to become their "Paris of the Far East" because of its beautiful and prosperous nature. Whatever the reason for its nickname, Saigon was my city of birth. It was the city that I was born and grew up in, and where I spent the first part of my life until it was taken over by communist forces on April 30th, 1975. The communists subsequently renamed it to Ho Chi Minh City, but for me and millions of other South Vietnamese, it will forever be Saigon.

Saigon during the late fifties and early sixties under the First Republic was peaceful: life was not rushed, and the "dong" had good value. I remember a bowl of Phở cost about five dong, which was about the same as the price for a movie ticket at a budget theater. My father made little money working as a government employee, but it was enough to support our family. When my sister Thu was born, he could hire a maid to help my mother out with work around the house. Every morning when he got ready to go to work, he turned on the radio to listen to the morning program and whistled to the tune of the song "Ngày Hạnh Phúc" (The Happy Day.) We would still be in bed, but we could still hear him whistling along with the song on the radio:

> Today the sky is light blue
> The wind gently caresses the dress tail,
> And the white clouds surround
> The pink sunrays illuminating the faith
> And young birds are dancing
> As they welcome the world's happy day
> Best wishes to those who found the port
> of dream... [14]

Every day, my father went home to eat lunch and take a nap before going back to work. Taking the afternoon nap had become a routine, and he also made us take it every afternoon. While taking a nap, he would turn on the radio to listen to the soft foreign music program of the Saigon radio station, which usually played the orchestra music from the great composer Paul Mauriat. The title track of the program is "A Summer Place," a song I heard every afternoon every time the radio was on. Even now, every time I hear this song, it always reminds me of those summer afternoons in the house where we grew up in the neighborhood of Phu-Nhuan. Later, there was also the "Foreign Music Request" program from the military radio station, where servicemen could request a song to play over the air. The program was broadcasted with a sweet southern accent:

> "And following is the song... according to the request
> of... at KBC (APO)..."

Songs like "Sealed with a Kiss," "Greenfields,"
"Pendant les Vacances," and "Too Young," among
others, followed me into the sweet afternoon naps.
During those years, Saigon was peaceful and a feeling of
happiness seemed to exist in every corner of the city.

When the government of Ngo Dinh Diem was
overthrown, the political situation in Saigon became
unstable. There was a vacuum of leadership at the highest
level, and demonstrations and protests were everywhere.
Then, the U.S. troops arrived, and lives of the people
were turned upside down as the war intensified. The price
of goods and services increased as people chased after the
dollar.

The Americans also changed the way people lived as
well as worked. They wanted the government to abandon
the siesta practice because they said a war cannot be
effectively fought when the government and the military
are taking afternoon naps. Since then, my father no
longer went home to eat lunch and take the afternoon nap
because his working hours were changed. But he came
home earlier, and he no longer worked on Saturday
mornings like before.

Saturday afternoons had always been special to us, as
we used to look forward to him coming home from work
to eat lunch and take a nap, and then when he woke up,
he would take us to the theater to see a movie and we
would eat out. Now everything had changed, in part

because everything had become more expensive, so going to see a movie and eating out were luxuries we could no longer afford. I remember mostly the peaceful and lazy afternoons of the city when all activities seemed to come to a standstill; the cyclo and taxi drivers napped inside their vehicles under the shades of the trees, and even the dogs found their places under the front porches to escape the summer heat. When the Americans came, they brought the noises of GMC trucks and jeeps along with a myriad of other vehicles. Saigon became noisier but also more active and bustling.

At the time, not many people had televisions in Saigon, and the only source of entertainment for each family was gathering around the radio to listen to the broadcast programs from the Saigon and military radio stations every evening. The military radio station in particular, had a program called "Voice of Dạ Lan." The "Dạ Lan" program comprised regular items such as news and music, but what was special about this program was the segment on the exchange of mails between the servicemen and the young women at home, which was read by "Dạ Lan." It was special because of the affectionate voice of "Dạ Lan," a voice that belonged to a young woman named "Xuân Lan" who was from the central region of Vietnam but broadcasted with a northern accent. Her segment touched the hearts of thousands of servicemen across the four military zones, especially those who were stationed at faraway outposts during the quiet and deserted nights, and brought warmness every night to the young soldiers through her sweet and personally affable voice:

"This is the Dạ Lan program, voices from the beloved home girls to our servicemen at the frontline."

After she left the program, "Phương Lan," another broadcaster with a no less affectionate voice, took over the program until South Vietnam collapsed in April 1975.

Besides the "Voice of Dạ Lan" which was designed for the servicemen of the ARVN, there was also a program called "Chiêu Hồi" which was designed to encourage defection by the Viet Cong and North Vietnamese soldiers to the side of the Republic of Vietnam government. As such, the program was broadcasted beyond the seventeenth parallel as part of the pacification effort and national reconciliation program. The "Chiêu Hồi" program, also known as "Tiếng Chim Gọi Đàn" (The Sound of Birds Calling) used the song "Ngày Về" (Return Day) by Hoàng Giác as the title track for the program:

Spread the wings and come back to the warm nest
Where everyday life is full of kindness,
Remembering the parting minute
when you hesitantly left
Regretting many of those younger days ... [15]

The selection of the song as the title track for the program by the South Vietnamese government had caused many problems for Hoàng Giác and his family in the North, even though he wrote the song back in 1946 when he was a member of the revolutionary propaganda team.

Although the program selected "Ngày Về" as its title

song, "Về Đây Anh!" (Come Back, Friend!) by Nguyễn Hiền and Nhật Bằng was specifically written for the "Chiêu Hồi" program. The lyrics of the song contained many passionate words to encourage soldiers on the other side to return "home" where their families were waiting for them. The lyrics were in stark contrast to the songs created by the communists, which often called for the killing and destruction of lives.

> Friend! Vietnam belongs to the Vietnamese
> Why are you fighting and tearing your hearts with hatred?
> Here's Bến Hải, the partition of two sides
> Stand up to search for the place of peace and happiness
>
> Friend! Why live a life of despair?
> Come back to protect and care for one another
> Here's the will of the people desperately waiting
> Why are you still indifferent?
>
> Friend! Come back and live a joyful life
> Where freedom is built for eternity,
> The bridge of love is bolstered everywhere
> Spring of peace is bustling over every man
>
> Friend! Wishing for a day when the fighting stops
> And everyone could live a peaceful life
> Here's a call to the old mother place faraway
> To those who are lost to come back here [16]

At exactly 10:00 pm each night, the voice of a female

broadcaster would gently remind everyone on the radio waves in a soft whisper:

"It is now 22:00 hours; please adjust the volume of your radio accordingly so that it does not disturb your neighbors who need quiet time to rest and enjoy their evening. Thank you for your consideration and cooperation."

All the radio programs of the First Republic showed the rich culture and sophisticated tradition of the free people of South Vietnam, which is something rarely seen in the capitalist-communist Vietnam society today.

For me personally, Saigon will also always be:

The rains that came and went unexpectedly.

The Saturday afternoons riding around town on my motorbike without the need to know where to go, but to just go.

The hot summer days wandering around town with friends on the streets lined with shaded trees.

The mornings, afternoons, and evenings at our favorite cafés to meet up with friends and to listen to the recent top hits from the U.S. and France.

The long days and months chewing on textbooks to study for the Baccalaureate exam, and hundreds of grams of Café de Martin and many sleepless nights.

The afternoons taking K.H. home after school on my Yamaha motorbike and stopping along the way to eat at the street vendor stands.

The trips taking my buddy to the Military Recruitment Office because he had received the draft paper, only to see him at our favorite café a couple of weeks later because he was temporarily disqualified because of his severe nearsightedness.

The summer afternoons standing with mom on the third floor of the Duy Tan apartment complex, looking down to the street below and listening to her stories about the old days in the North.

The evenings when the adults were playing mahjong downstairs, and I would climb up and lay on the rooftop of my grandparents' house to watch the falling stars and imagine I was the shepherd in the tale "Les Étoiles" from "Lettre de mon moulin" by Alphonse Daudet. The sky usually appeared to be profound, and the stars were indeed brilliant, but every once in a while, it was disturbed by the military flares that lit up the night.

The sound of the street vendors' callings and the noises of many vehicles from dusk till dawn. The familiar sound of the man selling Phở, the high-pitched voice of the woman selling sticky rice, and the clacking noise of the Chinese man selling noodle soup.

The Saigonese did not need a clock because the street vendors were always keeping them on time. In my neighborhood, every morning at exactly seven am and never a minute later, I would wake up to the sound of the woman selling French bread: "Bánh mì nóng hổi đây!" (Hot French bread here!).

A city for the movie lovers with many movie theaters, from low budget and affordable places where you could see two movies running consecutively, to upscale theaters like Rex and Mini Rex.

At the low budget theaters, you would not only get excitement from the movies you were watching but also from anything that might happen during the movie, such as the banging on the chairs if films got cut off in the middle, the rats running down below and up your legs, and sometimes the flying cigarette butts landing in your lap.

The upscale theaters, such as the Mini-Rex A & B, offered quite the opposite experience, where the air conditioning was always running extremely cold and the leather chairs were big enough for two people (ideally a couple) to cuddle together. The upscale theaters usually showed newer releases from Hollywood and France, while the low budget theaters always ran old movies including Indian or Chinese Kung Fu movies.

Saigon of the last days of the war was confusion and fear, the crowds panicking and rushing to the banks to make their last withdrawals, the long lines of people in front of the U.S. Embassy, the anxiety and fear of what lay ahead, the convoys of cars and trucks full of civilians and soldiers fleeing from the war zone and pouring into the city, the explosions of bombs and gun fires from Tan Son Nhut airbase the evening of April 28, the waves of people finding ways to leave the country at the port of Bach Dang, the image of the body of a soldier in his burnt jeep, the looks on the faces of the paratroopers who sat dejected on the curbside, their camouflage uniforms shed and littered all over the streets.

Saigon will forever be a part of me.

My mother, Ty Hoang
and my brother Thang.
(Do Family Archives)

My father, Victor Do and I.
(Do Family Archives)

My brother Thang
and I with our
father.
*(Do Family
Archives)*

My brother Thang and I at our
grandparent's house. Behind us is
the Mynah bird cage.
(Do Family Archives)

When Vice President Nixon visited Hanoi in 1953, my grandmother (black dress) escorted his wife, Pat for a tour of the city.

My grandparents at home. *(Do Family Archives)*

(Do Family Archives)

My grandfather's medals. OBE is on the left. *(Do Family Archives)*

My father at the National Zoo in Saigon, circa 1956. *(Do Family Archives)*

Me, circa 1959
(Do Family Archives)

Sitting with my grandfather in
one of the New Year (Tet)
pictures. *(Do Family Archives)*

Me with my family. Far left is my sister Thu, my brother Dai,
my sister Mai, my brother Cuong, and my little sister, Anh.
Standing in the back row: our mother, me, my brother
Thang, and our father. *(Do Family Archives)*

(L-R) My father, uncle Hop, uncle Kim, my grandmother, and my grandfather in Hanoi.
(Do Family Archives)

This building in Saigon was where the opium was manufactured during the first half of the 20th century.
(Source by manhhai via Flickr)

PRICE OF THE PRESIDENCY

The impeachment of President Donald J. Trump in 2019 for his abuse of power in pressuring the leader of a foreign country, Ukrainian President Volodymyr Zelensky, to pursue investigations of Joe Biden, a potential opponent in the 2020 presidential election at the time and his son Hunter Biden, reminded us of another political scandal in 1968 lest anyone forget.

The year 1968 was the height of the Vietnam War, the North Vietnamese communists and the Viet Cong had suffered major losses in the Tet Offensive. Psychologically, however, it was a turning point for the American public's support for the war. The public's opinion had already turned against President Johnson's Vietnam policies perhaps long before American broadcaster Walter Cronkite infamously reported that the war was lost, but it was exactly these words from Cronkite that convinced Johnson to declare that he would not run for a second term. "If I've lost Cronkite, I've lost middle

America," Johnson said in February 1968. The American people no longer wanted to support a long war that cost between $60 to $80 million dollars a day and an average casualty of 300 Americans dead a week. The anti-war movement had spread across the U.S. like wildfire and had prompted Johnson to announce his decision to halt the bombing of North Vietnam and to seek a solution to end the war at the peace talks in Paris.

The Republican nominee at the time, former Vice President Richard Nixon, was running with the pledge to have an honorable end to the war in Vietnam. Nixon was concerned that if South Vietnam President Nguyen Van Thieu proceeded with the peace accord before the election, it would affect his chance of winning the presidency. He secretly sent an envoy with a message to Thieu, advising him not to sign and to promise him a better deal if he became president. His personal representative was an American named Anna Chennault who helped Nixon win the presidency by persuading Thieu to boycott the peace talks, sabotaging Johnson's effort in reaching an agreement with North Vietnam to end the war. Johnson knew about the plot but did not make it public because he did not want the American people to think he did it to help Hubert Humphrey, his Vice President and the Democratic nominee. Privately, however, he told his aides Nixon's action amounted to "treason." Whether Nixon's conduct was treasonous is debatable, but clearly, he violated the Logan Act of 1779, which forbids a private citizen from corresponding with a foreign government without permission from the U.S. government.

Who was Anna Chennault and how did she get involved in what was later called "The Chennault Affair"? Anna Chennault was born Chen Xiangmei in Beijing in 1923. After she graduated from college in Hongkong, she worked as a wartime correspondent for the Central News Agency and met her future husband General Claire Chennault in 1944 during an assignment to interview him. General Chennault was the leader of the first American Volunteer Pilot Group called "Flying Tigers" who helped China defend against the Japanese aircraft during World War II. They fell in love and after World War II ended; he divorced his wife and married her. She moved to Washington, D.C. with her two young daughters after the general died of cancer in 1958 and started a new life by working as a reporter, translator, and consultant to U.S. companies seeking to expand their business in Asia.

During this period, she became popular among the Washington, D.C. social circles as the top fundraiser for the Republican Party through the events she organized at her penthouse in the Watergate. Yes, the same Watergate that attracted who is who of the U.S. political theater, including Richard Nixon, among others. She eventually served in his presidential campaign in 1968, and it was during this time that Nixon asked her to send a secret message to South Vietnam President Nguyen Van Thieu. For her work, Anna Chennault got little in return, as after Nixon got elected, he turned her down when she asked for a position as his Asian affair adviser. If she felt betrayed by Nixon, it was nothing compared with the price Thieu had to pay for trusting Nixon and helping him win the presidency.

The better deal Nixon promised Thieu was just a deception. After winning the election, Nixon announced his plan to Vietnamize the war, which meant that the U.S. would begin to withdraw U.S. troops gradually out of Vietnam, while increasing military supplies to South Vietnam to the point that it could fight the war without U.S. ground support. That was supposed to be the plan, but the real intention, however, was to create a "decent interval" so that it did not appear as if the U.S. just pulled the plug and abandoned its ally by withdrawing U.S. forces all at once.

In January 1972, Nixon revealed in a televised speech that Henry Kissinger, his National Security Adviser, had held a dozen secret peace negotiating meetings with North Vietnam from August 4, 1969, to August 16, 1971, without South Vietnam's participation and input. He also revealed the U.S. peace proposal was presented to the North Vietnamese, but that they rejected it.

The communists insisted on the withdrawal of U.S. and allied troops from all of Indochina with no conditions and the resignation of President Thieu. As the peace talks stalled, the communists launched a massive invasion of South Vietnam in March 1972, which was called the Easter Offensive as a test of Nixon's Vietnamization. Nixon responded by ordering the bombing of North Vietnam and increased air support for South Vietnamese forces to push back the communist attacks. In October of that year, in the wake of their failed offensive, Hanoi dropped the demand for Thieu to resign and was willing to consider serious negotiations with the U.S. again. This prompted Kissinger to declare prematurely that "peace was at hand," although Thieu had rejected the draft treaty prepared by Kissinger and Le Duc Tho, the North Vietnamese diplomat and member of Hanoi's politburo. Thieu was concerned - and rightly so, that the treaty would let Hanoi keep over 150,000 of its troops on South Vietnam soil.

His refusal to accept the deal had caused North Vietnam to walk out of the peace talk. Nixon was infuriated; he ordered another aerial bombing of North Vietnam, which was referred to as the Christmas bombing, to force Hanoi to get back to the negotiating table. The relentless bombing with hundreds of B-52 bomber sorties over the sky of Hanoi and over 20,000 tons of explosives on the capital city of North Vietnam brought the communist leadership back to the peace deal they had agreed to before they walked out.

The only remaining issue for Nixon was to get Thieu to accept the deal. He reassured Thieu that the U.S. would respond accordingly if North Vietnam violated the accord. Thieu knew that this would eventually lead to a complete takeover by the communists, but he had no choice, as Nixon had threatened to cut off military aid to Saigon if Thieu refused. "The Agreement on Ending the War and Restoring Peace in Vietnam" was signed by all sides a month later, on January 27, 1973. Nixon declared the peace accords as "Peace with Honor" but as Larry Berman described in his book "No Peace, No Honor", the only word that would accurately describe Nixon and Kissinger's actions toward their former ally is "betrayal."

Le Duc Tho, the North Vietnamese politburo member who declined the shared Nobel Peace Prize with Kissinger, knew there would be no peace, since the

communists had already planned to violate the peace
accords before the ink was even dry. According to
declassified records, the U.S. expected that the signed
treaty would be violated immediately, but that did not
stop Nixon from hailing it as "Peace with Honor" and
Kissinger from accepting his share of the Nobel Peace
Prize.

Nixon and Kissinger always maintained that the
treaty itself, while not perfect, allowed for a political
solution, had North Vietnam not blatantly violated it.
After Nixon's death in 1994, however, the government
declassified 2,636 hours of Nixon's secret tapes, which
confirmed that Nixon and Kissinger never believed
'Vietnamization' would actually work, as it only served
Nixon's political goals. Ken Hughes, a research specialist
with the University of Virginia's Miller Center, spent
more than a decade studying the tapes. He revealed in his
write-up "The Paris Peace Accords Were a Deadly
Deception" many damning findings about the peace
accords as deliberate fraud. He asserted, "These tapes
expose far worse abuses of power than the special
prosecutors ever found. After all, as the saying goes, no
one died in the Watergate. As commander-in-chief,
however, Nixon sacrificed the lives of American soldiers
to further his electoral ends."

On his first day in office, Nixon asked his top
advisors if South Vietnam could ever be able to fight the
communists on its own. They all said "never"; "even
when fully modernized," South Vietnam could not
survive "without U.S. combat support in the form of air,
helicopters, artillery, logistics and *major ground forces.*
These opinions turned out to be incorrect, as the ARVN

had proved that it could survive without U.S. ground forces, however, it could not survive without air support. No army in the world could fight off a major conventional attack without massive air support, including the U.S. Army; that was not even a fair assessment. Nonetheless, Nixon has his own plan. Based on the information from his advisors, he estimated South Vietnam would not last more than a year and a half, and that estimation formed the basis for the timeframe he needed - a "decent interval", as he called it. Publicly, Nixon continued to announce that the Vietnamization program was working and South Vietnam was making progress.

The whole concept of the deceptive Vietnamization policy was based on the presumption that South Vietnam could not survive without U.S. combat troops. According to Hughes, "In order to make it look successful, he spaced the troop withdrawals out across four years from over 500,000 in January 1969 to less than 50,000 by Election Day 1972."

The irony was that South Vietnam did, in fact, defeat the North Vietnamese Army without U.S. ground forces during the Easter Offensive in 1972, albeit with massive U.S. air support. The ARVN did all the fighting and dying, but this was lost with the U.S. media and the policy planners in Washington, D.C. South Vietnam forces fought against an enemy, who for the first time in the history of the Vietnam War, employed conventional warfare with tanks and modern weapons used by the regular infantry of the People's Army of Vietnam (PAVN) and backed by heavy artillery with unlimited supports from China and the Soviet Union. Even at the peak of the Vietnam War, when the U.S. had over 500,000 troops with all of its mighty air power and weaponry, the U.S. troops never had to face such a massive attack across the 17th parallel. This was evidence that Vietnamization actually worked if the U.S. continued to provide military aid and air support, and the "decent interval" would not even be necessary. But that would not help Nixon's political goal, as he had promised "peace with honor."

Nixon did not want to accept the reality that Vietnamization did work because he had provided assurance to China and Moscow that the U.S. would disengage and let the chips fall where they may. Otherwise, the U.S. would have to continue to provide military aid and air support to South Vietnam and the war would continue on. Congress and the American public would not support a war that had become unpopular and unsustainable. So, what would the solution be? What could Nixon do differently? Nixon could tell Kissinger to negotiate in good faith in South Vietnam's interest and demand Hanoi withdraw all their troops beyond the 17th parallel in order to guarantee a long-lasting peace. The U.S. did not have to give up South Vietnam in order to befriend China and the Soviet Union. Nixon could have used the U.S. power to pressure the two communist states to reign in North Vietnam and keep Vietnam as two separate countries like in Korea or Germany during the cold war. That was what President Johnson would have done, presumably, if Nixon had not interfered with the peace talks in 1968.

The tapes also revealed secret information regarding Kissinger's separate trips to China and the Soviet Union, where he promised China Premier Zhou Enlai and Soviet General Secretary Leonid Brezhnev that Nixon needed a cease fire for "say eighteen months" and after that if the communists overthrew the South Vietnamese government, the U.S. wouldn't intervene. He told them, "You have our assurance". In other words, he sold out South Vietnam to the communists. And so, 28 months after the "peace with honor" deal was signed in Paris, South Vietnam collapsed.

Thieu realized he should not have trusted Nixon, as he bet his country and lost. About a month before the fall of Saigon, Cambodia was also lost to the Khmer Rouge communists. One of its leaders, Prince Sirik Matak, also trusted the Americans and lost. He declined U.S. Ambassador John Gunther Dean's invitation to flee the country and seek political asylum in the United States. Hours before his execution on April 12, 1975, he wrote a letter to the ambassador:

Dear Excellency and friend,

I thank you very sincerely for your letter and for your offer to transport me towards freedom. I cannot, alas, leave in such a cowardly fashion.

As for you and in particular for your great country, I never believed for a moment that you would have this sentiment of abandoning a people which has chosen liberty. You have refused us your protection and we can do nothing about it. You leave us and it is my wish that you and your country will find happiness under the sky.

But mark it well that, if I shall die here on the spot and in my country that I love, it is too bad because we are all born and must die one day. I have only committed the mistake of believing in you, the Americans.

Please accept, Excellency, my dear friend, my faithful and friendly sentiments.

Prince Sirik Matak

No one knows better than Henry Kissinger, who in November 1968, said, "It may be dangerous to be America's enemy, but to be America's friend is fatal."

In the end, more than 27,000 Americans and millions of others died in vain in Indochina for the price of Nixon's presidency. He had promised "Peace with Honor" but there was no such peace and honor. History will never know if Thieu had declined Nixon's offer and accepted the peace deal in 1968; would it have made any difference? Would South Vietnam still exist as a free country today?

APRIL 30TH

Every year when April 30th comes, it always brings back many memories, like an old film being replayed in my head. After many decades, I've lost count of the exact number of years that have passed since the day the first Soviet made T-54 tank burst through the gates of the Independence Palace, but I will never forget that day. If December 7th, 1941 was the date which lived in infamy for the United States of America, then April 30th, 1975 was the date which lived in infamy for the people of South Vietnam. It marked the end of the Vietnam War and also wiped an entire country called The Republic of Vietnam (RVN) from the map of the world.

In April 1975, Saigon was on the verge of utter collapse. Twenty North Vietnamese Army (NVA) divisions were encircling the capital city. All efforts to find a political solution through the French Ambassador Jean Marie Merillon had failed since Hanoi smelled a total military victory and was in no mood for any negotiations.

On April 21ˢᵗ, President Thieu had resigned under pressure from Merillon and his generals to save Saigon. His Vice President, Tran Van Huong, took over, but he lasted only a week after the communists refused to recognize him. He then handed the position over to General Duong Van Minh, but by that time, negotiations were no longer possible.

The evening of April 28ᵗʰ, the communists fired a barrage of rockets into Tan Son Nhut Air Base to increase pressure on the Saigon government. From the third floor of our Duy Tan apartment building, I could see columns of black smoke rising from the direction of the air base. My brother Thang, who served in the Vietnam Air Force (VNAF) as a technical specialist, was stuck at the base and we had not heard from him for several days.

To appease Hanoi, the new lame duck president "Big Minh" ordered all Americans out of South Vietnam within 24 hours. On that day, thousands of people scaled the walls of the U.S. Embassy hoping to get evacuated by helicopters. Many people flocked to the harbor to look for a way out by ships. All hopes to get out by fixed-wing aircraft were no longer possible, as all runways were damaged by rocket fires and covered with debris, rendering them unfit for use.

The U.S. government had to proceed with Plan B for helicopter evacuation, which was called Operation Frequent Wind, to evacuate Americans and the Vietnamese who had worked for the U.S. The U.S. military radio station began playing Bing Crosby's "White Christmas" as a coded signal for all American personnel to move to their evacuation points. Under this plan, helicopters were used to fly Americans and Vietnamese refugees to the U.S. Navy aircraft carriers that were waiting off the coast. At Tan Son Nhut Air Base on the morning of April 29th, the commander of VNAF, Lieutenant General Tran Van Minh, and his staff went to the U.S. Defense Attaché Office (DAO) and requested to be evacuated to the USS Blue Ridge, leaving the base with no one in charge. My brother came home that morning looking lost and dejected. He had planned to take the family inside the base so that all of us could get out in one of the cargo planes in which he would bribe the crew members to let us go on board. But it was no longer feasible.

The next day, around noon on April 30th, President Minh announced "unconditional surrender" over national radio and called on all ARVN troops to cease fire and hostilities to prepare for an orderly handover of power to the communist provisional government.

Around this time, Thang and I were sitting jam-packed in our aunt's family car, heading to the Navy Yard. She had heard from her brother-in-law, Hưng, a Navy sailor, about a Navy ship that was damaged in a previous assignment and was not operational. According to Hưng, some Navy men were trying to repair it and he was unsure whether they would be successful, but it was a chance, nevertheless. My aunt Minh and her family had been staying at our apartment, hoping to find a mean to get out of the country. Her husband was a Colonel in the ARVN and had just been promoted to Commander of the infantry school in Thu Duc in early April to replace Lieutenant General Nguyen Vinh Nghi, who was reassigned to be commander of the III Corps Forward

Command to establish the defensive frontline at Phan Rang. As the situation worsened each passing day, however, he told her to take the children to Saigon and find a way to get out.

From our apartment building on Duy Tan Street, the small French made Renault packed with a dozen people made its way to the Duy Tan Square, which was also known as the Turtle Fountain. Along Duy Tan Street, the popular street lined with shaded trees where lovers used to come and walk arm in arm, was now littered with camouflage uniforms shed by Airborne troops. Once considered an elite branch of the ARVN, the Airborne division had been recalled from the battlefields to Saigon to protect the capital city, where they fought bravely against the advance of the NVA. After the "unconditional surrender" announcement, however, they felt betrayed. We saw some soldiers sitting on the sidewalk looking dejected, and a body in a burnt military Jeep as we passed by the front of Saigon University - some had blown themselves up with grenades.

As we approached the Notre Dame Cathedral, the car turned left onto Thong Nhat Boulevard. On the left was the U.S. Embassy, where just the day before, thousands of people tried to get inside to be evacuated; now, it looked deserted, with debris everywhere from the looting that occurred after the Americans left. Paper records, office furniture, miscellaneous equipment, and other items were littered all over the street.

As we passed the U.S. Embassy, we saw a column of tanks from afar approaching in our direction. Suddenly, everyone panicked since we did not know whether the tanks were ours or the NVA's. And if they were NVA tanks, would they stop us or fire at our car? My brother Thang quickly threw his military ID out of the car window as a precaution. As the rumbling noise of the tanks' engines and the sound of the tracks grinding on the asphalt surface of the street got louder and closer, I recognized the red and blue flag with a yellow star in the center: it was the flag of the Southern Liberation National Front (SLNF), a so-called organization created by the North Vietnamese Communist Party. We all held our breaths frantically. As the lead tank approached closer and closer, I saw "them", the Viet Cong, for the first time in my life.

They were sitting on the hull, with some on the turret of the tank with their AK-47 assault rifles in their hands. They looked rather strange and lost in their dirty green uniforms and their typical sun-helmets covered with jungle leaves. As their tanks passed by our car, they waved at us unexpectedly, and so quickly, we all waved back as if we had just been waved to by the Pope. However, they did not seem to pay much attention to us, and suddenly, I realized they had a much more important goal in mind: they were heading toward the Independence Palace. These were most likely the same tanks in which their images were later displayed on TV screens across the world when they crashed into the gates of the presidential palace.

After the tanks drove by our car, everyone felt a tremendous wave of relief, but we knew more dangers could wait ahead. The Renault slowly made its way to Nguyen Binh Khiem Street, turned right at the end of the intersection where the National Zoo was located, and headed toward the Naval Shipyard. I turned my head around and looked at the National Zoo's iron gate where, as children, our parents used to take us during the weekends, perhaps for the last time.

When we passed through the entrance to the Naval Shipyard, there were no guards at the gate. Inside, we saw people running in different directions and heard random gun shots everywhere. Unsure where to go, we drove around the base until we saw a lone ship by the dockyard. We could barely see a line of people on the gangplank.

From afar, the ship looked like a giant piece of old gray metal, just docked there, motionless and dormant. As we came closer, I saw the marking painted in white color on the front side of the ship that read "402." We followed the others and went onboard to find out if this would be the ship that would take us out of Saigon. As we went onboard, I was shocked to see thousands of people; civilians and military personnel already sitting shoulder to shoulder on the lower deck. We were told that people had been sitting there for hours, and no one knew whether the ship could be repaired, but no one wanted to leave either for fear that they might miss out on the last opportunity to escape. While we were looking around, we heard a NVA tank had just entered the Navy Yard. On the ship, everyone was told to stay in place and not make any moves or noise.

HQ 402 was a Landing Ship Medium (LSM) class used by the United States Navy during World War II. It was originally named USS LSM-226 and was first commissioned in November 1944, when it served in the Pacific theater during World War II until November 1945 and then decommissioned in July 1946. It was

recommissioned in September 1950 during the Korean
War, then decommissioned again in April 1954, and
transferred to France under the name RFS LSM 226.
The ship was finally transferred to the Republic of
Vietnam Navy in 1956 and was renamed HQ 402 *Lam
Giang*. This type of transport ship was used during the
evacuation of North Vietnamese people, mostly Catholic,
to the South, per the Geneva Convention Agreement in
1954. The Vietnamese refugees had nicknamed the ship
the "open-mouth ship" because of the bow doors at the
front of the ship that opened up. Perhaps HQ 402 was
one of those ships, and if so, wouldn't this be such a
coincidence? The same ship that transported Vietnamese
refugees escaping communism in 1954 would do so again
in 1975. Only in 1975, there would not be any welcome
signs that read "THIS IS YOUR PASSAGE TO
FREEDOM" like in 1954. If, in 1954, it was hope that
drove people to seek freedom, in 1975, it was despair and
fear.

Hours passed sitting inside the ship when a Catholic
priest told us that the Navy men were able to fix one
engine with one working generator, and we were going to
take our chances to depart from the dockyard. The priest
seemed to take on the role of a spiritual leader and
coordinator between the Navy men in charge and the
"passengers." He asked if anyone had a white piece of
clothing, such as a shirt, that could be raised up on the
upper deck so that the communists would not fire at our
ship as the gun turret of their tank was pointing in our
direction. Slowly, HQ 402 limped its way out to the
Saigon River. Everyone held their breaths, and some

people prayed in silence.

I looked at my watch; it was exactly 3:30 pm, April 30th, 1975.

LAST VOYAGE OF HQ 402

After leaving the Naval Shipyard, HQ 402 crawled on a single engine, zigzagging its way through the Saigon River, and heading in the direction of Nhà Bè towards the open sea. Sitting in a squatting position for so long, I did not know how many hours had passed, but I noticed it was getting dark. Everyone was quiet, perhaps preoccupied with their own thoughts and worries. Since leaving Saigon, my brother and I had not contemplated everything that happened, but sitting on that ship on our way out of the country, we finally had a moment to realize that we had just left behind our home, our parents, our brothers and sisters, and everything we had without knowing when we would ever see them again. We had planned to go back and pick them up, but the events that transpired at the base had prevented us from doing that, and so here we were on this handicapped ship, without knowing what the future would hold for us.

The voice of the priest suddenly pulled me back to reality. He informed everyone that we were about to pass Rừng Sát Special Zone, a well-known area controlled by the Viet Cong about twenty-two miles south-southeast of Saigon. This area was very dangerous and the Viet Cong could shoot or fire the B-40–a Chinese-made rocket-propelled grenade (RPG) - at our ship if they found out that we were trying to leave the country. He told everyone to be extremely quiet and to not make any sounds. By this time, the sky was totally dark and I could barely see the people around me inside the ship. As the ship waddled quietly through the Rừng Sát Special Zone, everyone held their breaths. Suddenly an orange dot lit up in the darkness, which appeared to come from a lit cigarette. Before anyone else could have any reaction, the high-pitched voice of a woman sitting near us immediately scorned the poor fellow:

"Stupid idiot! Do you want to kill all of us?"

"Everyone, please be quiet, shush!"

I heard other people trying to calm the woman down, and the orange dot went out as quickly as it came on. I could not help but wonder what the fellow was thinking when he lit up a cigarette at a wrong time and about the manner of the woman with the high-pitched voice. It showed that only when facing with life and death, the true characters of people would reveal.

Eventually, our ship made it through the danger area with no incident. After a long day with so much anxiety, I felt exhausted and tired, still sitting in a somewhat squatting position with my butt on the floor. Because there was no room for me to stretch my legs out, I crossed my arms above my knees to rest my head and fell asleep.

When I woke up, the morning sunlight had broken through and lit up the entire lower deck. I looked around and saw people everywhere, some walking around, since perhaps we were no longer in imminent danger. My brother told me we had just passed Vung Tau, and we were heading to Con Son Island to meet up with other Vietnamese naval ships.

Con Son Island was well known during the French colonial period as a penal colony, similar to the French Guiana, which became famous in the movie Papillion. It was called Grande-Condore by the French and Pulo Condore by the English. Marco Polo mentioned the island on his 1292 voyage from China to India as both Sondur and Condur. The prison on the island was built in 1861 by the French colonists to hold political prisoners deemed dangerous to the colonial government, and was later turned over to the South Vietnamese government in 1954. The nationalist and reformer Phan Chu Trinh was jailed at Con Son from 1908 to 1911. Other notable prisoners included communist leaders Ton Duc Thang, Pham Van Dong, and Le Duc Tho.

Since we left the previous day, we had nothing to put in our stomachs, and I felt hungry like never. It was probably the first time in my life that I had ever felt that hungry. Suddenly, I realized that May 1st was my 19th birthday, and I remembered the bottle of wine that I had saved for the special occasion, which I would never get to drink, and I just let out a dry laugh. No cake and no wine. I just wished for some food or anything to calm my stomach.

Just a couple of days before, my friend Toan and I

had been at Van Hanh University's campus when we learned all classes had been cancelled, so we wandered around the city to glimpse the mood of the people in the streets. We could feel that there was a somber atmosphere that was enveloping the entire city; everyone seemed to be in a hurry. We could see the anxiety and fear and despair on people's faces. We stopped by our favorite café, La Pagode, in downtown Saigon. The place was unusually empty, and we had no problem finding a table, since everyone was probably out trying to leave the country. From where we sat, I could see the historic Hotel Continental across the street on the far right. This was the place where Graham Greene had written his acclaimed novel "The Quiet American" in 1955 on the café terrace of the hotel.

While we were sitting at La Pagode, we heard on the radio that North Vietnamese pilots and VNAF defectors had bombed Tan Son Nhut Air Base using captured VNAF A-37 aircraft. The group was led by first lieutenant Nguyen Thanh Trung, who had defected weeks earlier on April 8th when he flew an F-5E from Bien Hoa Air Base and dropped two bombs on the Independence Palace. Luckily, one bomb hit the ground and caused minor damages, but no casualties, and the second bomb failed to explode.

As we were about to leave, the sky suddenly became dark with lightning and rumbling thunder. The thunder was so loud that it rocked the place as if it was being hit by a bomb from the enemy aircraft. Then the storm came, and the rain poured down heavily as I had never seen before. And it continued for hours as if God were crying for a beloved city that was about to fall into the devil's hands. Coincidentally, a CCR song, "Who'll Stop the Rain" was being played in the background from the restaurant's music tape recorder. Neither Toan nor I found the sun on that day as Fogerty was chanting in the song, and little did we know that was the last time we would see each other again until thirty-seven years later, as our lives would change forever only a few days later.

As I replayed in slow motion everything that happened on that day over and over in my head, several small boats approached our ship and demanded to come on board. The small boats were full of South Vietnam Marines. After they went on board, the Navy men asked them to turn over their weapons, but they refused. After back-and-forth negotiations turned into an altercation between the men, the newcomers agreed to throw their guns overboard. Thankfully, the situation ended peacefully, with no escalation.

It is worth noting here that HQ 402 had no captain. It was the last ship that was left at the Naval Shipyard because it was inoperable. In March 1975, during its last mission, the ship was damaged because of enemy rockets when it tried to rescue SVN Marines in Da Nang, and transported the troops to Cam Ranh, and finally to Vung Tau, before it returned to Saigon for major overhaul. A group of Navy men had barely repaired it at the last minute and operated it. As I researched for more information about HQ 402, I learned that a lieutenant named Cao The Hung, who worked on fixing the ship tirelessly and unselfishly with others, to take all of us out to the ocean. It was perhaps a combination of both perseverance and miracle that Hung and other men could repair it under such enormous pressure. We owed these men a great deal of debt. I don't know them personally, but I want to take this opportunity to express my deepest appreciation for everything they did that day. They were: Lieutenant Cao The Hung, Lieutenant Nguyen Huu Thien, Lieutenant Luu An Hue, Lieutenant Nguyen Van Thuoc, and many others whom I might have missed.

When HQ 402 got close to Con Son Island, the damaged bow doors in front of the ship started to take on water. People below deck were bailing out water with everything they had. They called on other men for help. Looking around, I caught the eyes of a middle-aged woman who was staring in our direction. She was saying something to someone with a high-pitched voice; I immediately thought of the woman from the night before who scolded the poor smoker. Without hesitation, my brother and I stood up and went to help.

But there was nothing we could do as we were told HQ 402 was in immediate danger of sinking. The Navy men sent signals to other ships nearby for help. Subsequently, several people from a U.S. Navy ship came on a crew boat and went on board to assess the situation. They determined HQ 402 was not savable and everyone would need to be transferred to other ships as soon as possible.

At the time, I thought HQ 402 was a lone ship that got out at the last minute and that all other ships had already been long gone the day before. I did not know that it was actually a coordinated effort between Richard Armitage, a young thirty-year-old civilian, and Capt. Kiem Do, deputy chief of staff for the South Vietnamese Navy, to have the South Vietnam naval ships gather at Con Son Island and wait for assistance from the U.S. Navy.

Armitage was on a special assignment from the Secretary of Defense to rescue the Vietnamese Navy; he had been a Navy intelligence officer working with the South Vietnamese units before he resigned in protest of the signing of the Paris Peace Accords, as he felt Nixon had sold out South Vietnam.[17] Armitage was on board the USS Kirk, a small destroyer escort, which had the lead role to coordinate and assist with the rescue effort. On that day, the USS Kirk was at Con Son Island, about fifty miles off the coast of South Vietnam, and was ready to assist HQ 402 with lifeboats and medical personnel.

With USS Kirk on standby, HQ 03 *Tran Nhat Duat*, the South Vietnamese flagship, came alongside HQ 402 and transferred the refugees by jury-rigged planks to the larger ship. The priority was for women, children, and the elderly to transfer first, but a man impatiently jumped and pushed a woman in front of him, causing her to fall into the ocean. We heard a Vietnamese Navy officer who was coordinating the transfer, pull out a pistol and shoot the man dead right in the head. We did not know whether they could save the woman who fell off the ship, but it was a tragedy to witness.

When HQ 03 was full and could not take on any more passengers, other ships came along to continue to transfer more people to their ships. They included HQ 02, *Tran Quang Khai*, a large Patrol Craft (PC), and HQ 06, *Tran Quoc Toan*, a battleship. While everyone was lining up to go to other ships, we just waited patiently. We were not worried, as we knew we would be eventually rescued. Finally, we were among the last group of people who were transferred to HQ 11 *Chi Linh*, a Dragueur Yard Mine Sweeper (YMS).

When everyone was safely onboard, and HQ 11 had pulled away, HQ 402 was subsequently scuttled outside of Con Son Island. From the upper deck of HQ 11, we saw HQ 402 for the last time, as it was slowly going under. The ship had survived through many wars: World War II, Korean War, and the Vietnam War. It finally found its resting place at the bottom of the ocean outside of Con Son Island. Standing on HQ 11, we all said farewell quietly to HQ 402, the ship that took us out of Vietnam and to freedom. It was estimated between 3,000 to 5,000 refugees were on board HQ 402 and who were successfully rescued by other ships.

Many stories had been written about the ship HQ 402, including the PBS documentary film "Last Days in Vietnam" by director Rory Kennedy in 2014.[18]

JOURNEY TO FREEDOM

On board HQ 11, we could walk around. There was room for everyone to sit or lay down so we did not have to sit in squatting positions like on HQ 402. Everyone received a pack of instant ramen noodles, but since there was no hot water to cook the noodle, we just ate it straight out of the bag. At that point, anything to fill our stomachs tasted good. I noticed most people on the ship were military members, but there were also civilians like me and women and children.

During the days we were on the ship, the ocean was perfectly calm. At night, my brother and I found a quiet secluded area above the upper deck by the twin-gun shield mount. It was a perfect place to sleep away from the crowd. We could watch the stars above and enjoy the cool, fresh ocean air. It was during these moments that we wondered about our family back in Saigon; what would happen to them, and were they going to be alright? Saigon seemed so far away in those moments.

In the morning when we woke up, we watched the sunrise from the horizon afar and realized just how tiny a human being was in the vast ocean. When the sun was up and we could see more clearly around us, we noticed a completely different picture. The USS Kirk and other U.S. Navy ships from the Seventh Fleet escorted a flotilla of about thirty VN Navy ships extended across the horizon, as far as the eye could see. It was a scene I thought I would only see in World War II movies set in the Pacific. In a way, I felt humbled to be a witness to the historical event of the entire South Vietnam's Navy being rescued by the U.S. Seventh Fleet.

I lost track of how many days we had been at sea when we neared Subic Bay, a U.S. Naval Base in the Philippines. Subic Bay was a large facility; its entire base, including the Subic Special Economic and Freeport Zone and military reservations, was almost the size of Singapore at about 300 square miles. During the Vietnam War, it became the U.S. Seventh Fleet forward base for repair and replenishment of naval ships. It also received visits from Military Sea Transportation Service ships bringing food, ammunition, supplies, fuel oil, aviation gasoline and jet fuel to transfer to Clark Air Base via a 41-mile pipeline.[19]

When we arrived at Subic Bay, the Philippines government refused to allow us entering the base. Apparently, the Philippines president, Ferdinand Marcos, did not want to offend the new government of Saigon because, according to him, South Vietnam had lost the war and thus the ships should belong to the communist government. Marcos was one of the first people to

recognize the communist ruler of the unified Vietnam
and wanted the ships to go back to Vietnam. During the
Vietnam War, the Philippines was an ally of both the U.S.
and South Vietnam, but now Marcos was quick to turn us
away. Although South Vietnam was no longer a country,
the U.S. was still an ally of the Philippines and was paying
the Philippines more than $300 million per year for the
lease and use of the base. Therefore, the U.S. should
have had the right to bring the ships into its own base, so
you would think.

While the U.S. was negotiating with Marcos, over 30
ships from the Vietnam Navy with tens of thousands of
refugees on board waited off the coast. Hours passed, and
the evening came and there was still no word from
Marcos. Standing on the upper deck of HQ 11, we could
see the lights around the base illuminating it from afar and
we wondered if the lights in Saigon would be on at that
same moment.

The next morning, we received news that Marcos
had finally agreed to let the ships come into the Naval
Base with the condition that the South Vietnam flags on
all 30 ships had to be replaced with U.S. flags and all
weapons had to be dumped into the ocean before
entering the base. Decades later, I learned it was Armitage
and Kiem Do who came up with this solution that Marcos
had to accept. The idea behind this solution was these
ships were on loan from the U.S. to South Vietnam
during the war and now that the war had ended, the ships
were being returned to the U.S. government, therefore
South Vietnam flags would be replaced with U.S. flags.
We also did not know at the time that there was a frantic
search to find thirty U.S. flags, but somehow the Navy

officers from USS Kirk were able to collect them among other U.S. ships and from the base.

On HQ 11, we were asked to help carry ammunitions of all sorts: 20 mm, 40 mmm and 80 mm from the lower deck and dump them overboard. On the main deck, small firearms and other weapons were stacked into big piles and then thrown into the ocean. As per the agreement between the U.S. and the Philippines government, each ship would have a U.S. Navy officer in command to bring it into port as U.S. ship with the U.S. flag flying. But before handing over command of the ships to the Americans, a somewhat formal ceremony to lower the South Vietnam flag would occur on each ship.

Rick Sautter, one of USS Kirk's officers who took command of a Vietnamese Navy ship, said,

"That was the last vestige of South Vietnam. And when those flags came down and the American flags went up, that was it. Because a Navy ship is sovereign territory and so that was the last sovereign territory of the Republic of Vietnam."

On HQ 11, we all gathered around the main deck to witness the lowering of the South Vietnam flag, and as it was coming down, we all sang our national anthem. Everyone was crying. When it was over, there was a commotion near the flagpole and someone shouting for help. We heard someone say there was a young woman who had apparently taken a large dose of quinine to end her life. The U.S. Navy officer onboard radioed a team of medics to come in a small boat to take the young woman back to their ship. Everyone was praying for her and hoping that she would be ok.

Sadly, it seemed the young woman had died as we

watched from the deck on HQ 11; several U.S. sailors lowered what appeared to be a body bag into the ocean. It looked like they had just performed some kind of burial at sea. All I could remember was that she had long, black hair and was wearing a white shirt and black pants. I was taken aback and saddened by the tragic event and could only hope she found peace. Though her journey had ended, for us it was only the beginning.

And so, on May 7, the fleet of Vietnamese Navy ships flying American flags finally entered Subic Bay. Upon debarking from HQ 11, we were moved to a pier and immediately transferred to a Military Sealift Command (MSC) ship for transportation to Guam. I was really impressed and thought that the transfer of thousands of refugees by the U.S. Navy personnel in such a short time frame was well organized and proficient.

As we were going up the gangplank to go onboard the big merchant ship, I looked around and saw a group of shirtless G.I.s working from afar, looking like red boiled shrimps under the hot Pacific sun. The smell of burning diesel from the GMC trucks running nearby reminded me of much of the war we had just escaped from. The picture of the massive naval base with rows of battleships along with the sounds of F5 aircraft flying above the sky from the nearby Clark Air Base demonstrated to us that the U.S. war machine was as powerful as ever. It was not the picture of a country that had just lost a war, as politicians in Washington wanted everyone to believe. Don't be fooled by what was said in history books; the U.S. did not win the war, but it did not lose it either. It just called it quit when the war no longer served its interest and purpose.

Leaving Subic Bay, the merchant ship headed toward Guam, where the U.S. authorities had established a refugee center in Orote Point weeks earlier in anticipation of the fall of Saigon and the evacuation of Vietnamese war refugees. Guam is a U.S. territory in the Western Pacific Ocean, about 1,300 nautical miles east of the Philippines. It is a major strategic asset of the U.S. military in the Pacific. The Navy Construction Battalions (CB), nicknamed Seabees, had received an order on April 22nd to construct a "tent city" and refurbish the Asan annex of the Navy's regional medical center to receive the refugees.

The day before April 22, President Nguyen Van Thieu had ordered a retreat of the ARVN 18th Division towards Saigon from Xuan Loc for the defense of the capital. The 18th Division under General Le Minh Dao had beaten off several NVA attempts to take the town of Xuan Loc and stalled its advance, but it was ultimately outnumbered and overwhelmed by the communist forces. It was the last major battle of the Vietnam War. President Thieu went on national TV and radio that day to announce his resignation and denounce the United States as betrayers. He promised to continue to stay and fight as a soldier but five days later in the darkness of the early morning; he was transported to Tan Son Nhut Air Base in a limousine driven by CIA Frank Snepp where an U.S. Air Force C-118 was waiting on the tarmac to take him to Taiwan. Included with Thieu's entourage were Prime Minister Tran Thien Khiem and several South Vietnamese senior aides.[20]

On April 23rd, during a speech at Tulane University,

as the North Vietnamese troops were surrounding Saigon for the final assault, President Gerald Ford announced the Vietnam War was finished as far as America was concerned despite previous promises by Ford and Nixon to support South Vietnam,

"Today, Americans can regain the sense of pride that existed before Vietnam. But it cannot be achieved by re-fighting a war."

The truth was the U.S. had anticipated this day since 1973 with the signing of the Paris Peace Accords. Simply put, this tragedy was planned. We were considered the lucky ones, who were able to get out, but at what price?

During the days on board the merchant ship, everyone huddled against the Pacific sun on the main deck under large canvas awnings temporarily set up by merchant sailors. We had water hoses for washing and cleaning but they were out in the open, so the children use them to cool off during the hot days more often than they were used for cleaning, while women were reluctant to use them under the staring eyes of merchant sailors who were watching from the upper deck.

To solve the problem of bathrooms for thousands of refugees, makeshift cubicle toilets of wooden slats and canvas covers were built to hang over the ship's railing and over the water. Because the canvases covered the side facing the ship, when nature called, we would have to go around to the side facing the ocean to find an empty spot among others who were squatting and taking care of their business. I never thought going to the bathroom was such a dangerous but necessary adventure. It was always very windy on the main deck, and the canvas did not hold up very well against the wind, so young women, especially, went in pairs so that one person could stand outside and hold the canvas in place for the other. When the wind was strong, it carried the stink in toward the people who were camping at the end of the ship. It was horrible, but who was complaining? We were provided with sufficient food, water and occasionally fruit, so our journey went smoothly with no incidents or drama. Finally, we arrived in Guam on May 15.

Upon our arrival, military personnel led us to a Naval Depot where we completed our refugee registration forms and received general medical checkups. The International Red Cross then interviewed and asked us where we would want to resettle. When we left Saigon, we never thought about where we would go; we just wanted to get out and go anywhere that we would not have to live under communist rule. Thus, when we were asked, the first country that came to mind was France, because our uncle lived there.

Afterward, yellow buses transported us to the "tent city" in Orote Point, which was actually a maze of thousands of tents put up in every direction. We were assigned to a tent with about ten other refugees. Each one of us was provided with a cot and a green military blanket.

We would have two meals a day served by the U.S. military. The lines were always about a mile long under the hot and burning sun, which did not help when tensions flared, as they often did, between the G.I.s working at the kitchen tent and the refugees. The reason for this tension was because some of the G.I.s treated refugees like inmates or beggars. Most of the G.I.s were nice and professional, but some were just terrible. Once, after waiting in line under the hot sun for hours to receive a spoon of food dumped on their plates and being told to go back out under the sun and get in line again if they wanted more food, some former ARVN soldiers were infuriated especially when the G.I.s told them to "di di mau", a phrase they learned in Vietnamese to tell people to go away quickly. The former soldiers torn down the tent kitchen in protest. The M.P. (Military Police) was called in to handle the situation. Afterward, the condition was significantly improved, and we were treated much better, more humanly perhaps.

Occasionally, a group of refugees went into the nearby woods to look for some plants to cook the homemade soup they long missed. One day, some men fell sick after eating some poisonous plants and had to be treated in the camp hospital. Luckily, no one was seriously hurt. After the incident, the camp commander no longer allowed the refugees to go into the woods to look for food.

Several weeks passed before the International Red Cross notified Thang and I that they could not locate our uncle in Paris. They said Paris is a big city, and without an exact address, it would be almost impossible to find him. We were told we had no choice but to go to the U.S. This turned out to be the best choice that we did not even make ourselves. We did not know at the time how difficult it was for someone with no connection in the U.S. to go to a place that could only be a dream for others. However, the refugee camps in the U.S. mainland such as Camp Pendleton in California, Fort Chaffee in Arkansas and Eglin Air Force Base in Florida were all strained to capacity, so we had to wait until the U.S. could build out more spaces at those facilities.

Meanwhile, life in the tent city seemed to settle into a routine; we spent the days getting in long lines for meals, and walking around and exploring the area although we were not permitted to go outside of the tent city. By this time, the refugee camp population had reached nearly 48,000, it had begun to develop some typical social problems, such as crimes and prostitution. There were reports of theft by bands of youths or former soldiers and some G.I.s were involved with some Vietnamese sex workers who used to work around the port of Bach Dang in Saigon. For a while, business of the oldest profession seemed to thrive when night time came at the camp. M.P.s in white helmet would drive around in their jeeps to conduct frequent patrols and to stop these illegal activities as much as possible. To keep the refugees out of trouble, entertainment, such as outdoor movies every night, was set up at designated places throughout the camp. They were mostly Bugs Bunny cartoons and old movies.

For those who had money, they could go shopping at the Post Exchange (PX) normally reserved for G.I.s only. I was surprised to see that many people carried a lot of dollars with them; many brought gold with them from Vietnam, which they could sell at PX for cash and buy things I would consider "luxury" items for a refugee. I would feel a twinge of envy for their fortune. One day someone gave me a quarter, and it was a fortune for me since you could buy either a pack of Pall Mall or a can of Coke from vending machines at PX. It was an easy choice for me; I knew I could quench my thirst during a hot summer day for a few minutes with a soda, but as a casual smoker, a pack of cigarettes could last me at least several weeks during cool nights watching Bugs Bunny cartoons on the beach.

When we had left Saigon, we brought nothing with us other than the clothes on our backs and our identification papers. We had some Vietnamese money, but they were worthless. Once in a while, the Red Cross had a truck loaded with used clothing donated by local charities come to the camp. The truck usually came around mid-morning at the intersection of the camp's two major streets, which the refugees called it "International Intersection" for some reason I never knew. We tried to go there a few times, hoping to get something, or at least a shirt, we could change into, but we never had any luck. The clothes were usually too big for us as the smaller sizes ran out quickly. Perhaps, if we skipped lunch and went out really early to get in line, we could have found something usable to wear but we always ended up deciding against it since there was no guarantee we could find something, and we did not want to miss our lunches.

Among the refugees, there were about 1,600 people, mostly military and naval personnel, who wanted to go back to Vietnam. They said they were forced to evacuate against their will and leave behind their families. Repatriation needed cooperation from the communist government in Vietnam, but efforts to get a response out of Vietnam went nowhere. As the process dragged on, the refugees became more restless. They staged demonstrations, some shaved their heads and went on a hunger-strike. One of those people involved was my cousin's husband, a lieutenant of the South Vietnamese Navy. He was on a battleship that went out to sea during the evacuation and ended up in Guam. His wife and child were still in Saigon and did not know what had happened to him. I ran into him while walking around the camp and he told me that he and some of the other men were planning to go back at all costs.

The U.S. eventually agreed to let the men depart for Vietnam on their own aboard the merchant ship Vietnam Thuong Tin. The U.S. Navy fixed up the ship and provided them with enough fuel and supplies for a round trip in case they had any problems and needed to return to Guam. No one knew the fate of the ship for more than a decade. Many years later, I received news from my cousin that after her husband and everyone on the ship arrived in Vietnam; the communists would not let them disembark and keep them off the coast for days without knowing what would happen to them. When the communists finally allowed them to come on shore, they immediately loaded them into military trucks and sent them to labor camps for over ten years. When my cousin's husband was released, he took his wife and child and escaped to Australia where they now live. The ship's captain, Tran Dinh Tru, also told his story later, sharing that he was imprisoned for 12 years.

As Summer arrived, we were notified of a new refugee camp opening in Pennsylvania and anyone who wanted to volunteer to sign up could leave for the U.S. rather quickly. Since everyone, including our aunt and her family, wanted to wait for Camp Pendleton in California because they preferred the warm weather there, which meant that we could end up waiting for a while in Guam. We had heard the tent cities at Camp Pendleton, the huge marine base in California, were jammed with over 18,000 refugees. The situation at Fort Chaffee, with about 10,000 refugees, was also similar; it had already exceeded the expected capacity of over 2,000. And Eglin base in Florida also had no more vacancies. My brother and I decided we would sign up to go to Fort Indiantown Gap in Pennsylvania, as we did not mind the cold weather.

Everything happened quickly after that. Within a couple of days, a yellow bus transported us and other "volunteers" to a hangar at Andersen Air Force Base about 59 miles north of Orote Point to spend the night and wait for our flight out the next morning.

Andersen Air Force Base was one of the four U.S. Air Force Bomber Forward Operating Locations in the Western Pacific and was home to B-52 bombers during the Vietnam War. The B-52s at Andersen and other bombers stationed at U-Tapao in Thailand took part in regular bombing missions over Vietnam until 1973, when the Paris Peace Accords were signed. During the months leading to the fall of Saigon, the one thing that worried the North Vietnamese politburo the most was the B-52s. The absence of the B-52s would mean that the U.S. would not intervene and served as a signal for the communists to push ahead. And of course, the B52s did not return to the battlefields in Vietnam, as they were sitting here at Andersen AFB.

When we arrived at Andersen AFB, I saw hundreds of B-52s impressively sitting in rows like sleepy giant black birds on the airfield. The B-52, known as the "Flying Fortress' or by its nickname "Big Ugly Fat Fucker" (BUFF), could carry up to 70,000 pounds of bombs and could fly over 8,000 miles at altitudes up to 50,000 feet without aerial refueling. With eight turbojet engines and a wingspan larger than the width of a football field, the B-52 was a nightmare for the North Vietnamese troops. Each of the 500- to 750- pound bombs could create a crater about the size of a swimming pool.

According to declassified information, the North Vietnamese confessed that had the U.S. continued the B-52 bombing of Ha Noi during operation Line Backer II in December 1972 for another week, the communists would have surrendered unconditionally but alas, that was not Nixon's goal. His goal was not to achieve military victory but to score a political goal in forcing North Vietnam to go back to the negotiating table.

By this time, everyone realized the Paris Peace Accord was just a ticket for the U.S. to get out of Vietnam; Nixon had no intention of the U.S. to intervene if the communists violated the agreement despite his promises to Thieu. I would not be surprised if Kissinger had also promised to China that the U.S. would not intervene should China attack and take the Paracel islands from Vietnam. This would explain why the U.S. Seventh Fleet denied the request for help from South Vietnam Navy in 1974 during the battle of the Paracel Islands between the naval forces of China and South Vietnam even though there was an U.S. liaison officer on assignment with South Vietnamese Navy. Gerald Emil Kosh, a former U.S. Army captain who was onboard one of the South Vietnamese battleships and was captured as a prisoner along with the South Vietnamese by the Chinese. According to the Associated Press (AP):

"The United States is taking a strictly hands off policy in the dispute between the Communist China and

South Vietnam over the Paracel Islands in the South China Sea."

"We have no claims ourselves and we are not involved in the dispute," said department spokesperson John King.

"It is for the claimants to solve among themselves."

King said the United States had no independent direct knowledge that China had landed troops on the islands. I seriously doubt that China would be bold enough to take those islands from South Vietnam if there were not some sort of agreement beforehand with the U.S.

That night, as I was lying on the bunk bed in the hangar at Andersen AFB, I was not sure if everything that happened since we left Saigon was just a dream or if it was really happening. I thought about our family, the harrowing journey, the long lines under the hot burning sun, the nights watching cartoon movies on the beach, and the times walking on the dirt roads around the camp and encountering gigantic frogs about the size of a foot. Somewhere from a cassette player, the sound of an antiwar song I used to listen to in Saigon by a popular folks' singer suddenly annoyed me as I tried to fall asleep.

As the commercial airplane was taking off, I looked out the window and saw below hundreds of B-52s still sitting on the airfield silently and obediently until they would be called upon in the next war. Finally, we were on our way to America. A feeling of bitter-sweetness settled upon us as we were anxious for the new life that awaited us, but we were also sad and worried for our family and the people who were still left behind.

THE TWO FRIENDS

I met Nguyen H. Hoai and Le T. Tin. at Fort
Indiantown Gap in the summer of 1975. Like other
refugees who were in the same situation without family,
we quickly became close friends. Hoai was a 40-year-old
Army Medical Doctor. During the last days of the war,
when his unit was disintegrated, he was forced to evacuate
and could not go home to pick up his wife and child. Tin
was a 19-year-old young man from My-Tho, and he too
lost contact with his family and came to the U.S. alone.

Fort Indiantown Gap, or the "Gap," as it is
commonly called, is in Lebanon County, Pennsylvania,
near Interstate 81, about 23 miles northeast of
Harrisburg. During the Vietnam War, it served as one of
the largest Reserve Officers' Training Corps (ROTC)
summer camps for the U.S. Army. In 1975, the Gap also
served as the third refugee camp for Southeast Asian
refugees, mostly from Vietnam. The other two refugee
camps were Camp Pendleton in California and Fort
Chaffee in Arkansas. My brother and I arrived at the Gap

in late June, when the weather was warm and not as humid. We were among the 32,000 Vietnamese and Cambodian refugees who arrived there throughout the summer of 1975.

The Gap is a large Army Base comprising 15 areas, with Areas 4 and 6 designated as temporary shelters for the refugees. It would be our home for the foreseeable future until a family or an organization could sponsor us. There were shuttle buses going back and forth between the two areas, but the areas were also within walking distance of each other, so we usually walked to attend different activities or to look for acquaintances. Each area comprised three or more rows of two-story white barracks with gray roofs. Inside the barrack, each level was partitioned into units separated by panel dividers where one or more families or groups would share the space of one unit or "room".

We were assigned to one of the white barracks in Area 6. Since there were only two of us, we had to share the "room" with other families. We each had our own bed and although it was a bunk bed, it was still a significant improvement from the green cot bed we slept on in Guam. We had an interesting group of "roommates" from completely different backgrounds. Across from our bed was a family from a fishing village near Vung Tau. The parents had a son around ten years old and a teenage daughter. Next to our bed was a Catholic priest who was also a professor of philosophy at the University of Saigon, named Luong K. Dinh, and his two disciples. He was a renowned scholar who had published over 40 books on Vietnamese culture and philosophy. And of course, there were me and my

111

brother, a university student from Saigon and a technical specialist from the Vietnam Air Force (VNAF).

Each barracks had a large public bathroom shared by both men and women. When nature called, it was common to find yourself sitting in a bathroom stall next to a member of the different sex, but you got used to it, because if you had to go, you had to go. The bathroom also had a communal shower area. Usage was allotted in a two-hour timeframe, alternating throughout the day for each gender group. Unfortunately, accidents happened every once in a while, when someone walked in while other people from the opposite gender were still in the middle of their showers. To be on the safe side, we had to announce ourselves loudly before entering, in case someone did not pay attention and stayed beyond their allotted timeframe. But that only solved the problem for women and not for us, so when I was in the shower, I usually whistled loudly to make my presence known. My favorite song was "Colonel Bogey March" which is the tune whistled by British POWs in the 1957 film "The Bridge on the River Kwai".

We were also responsible for taking turns to maintain the public bathroom area. My particular task was to check the bathroom supplies, such as soaps and toilet papers, keep track of the inventory, and go to the main office to get fresh supplies as necessary. One night, I had to go up to the second level, where the supply items were kept to get some toilet paper rolls to bring down to the bathroom. The room was dark, and I stumbled onto the bunk bed, which was used to store the supplies. It was at that moment I saw a silhouette of someone on the bed, and as my eyes adjusted to the darkness, I saw it was actually two persons; a guy and a girl making out with each other. Suddenly I recognized the girl. She was the teenage daughter of the fisherman from our "room" downstairs. I was taken aback for a moment, but then I just left. "None of my business," I said to myself. Encounters like that occurred more often than not at the Gap since there was not a lot of privacy when many people lived together and shared the same space inside a barracks with no doors.

I met a young woman who used to be a hooker in Saigon, and the day the city fell, she was hanging around near the harbor and saw a ship that was about to depart, so she climbed aboard the ship and ended up here at the Gap. Life inside the Gap was like a mini version of society outside, where you would meet all different people from all different walks of life. That was how I met Hoai and Tin; specifically, I met Tin at a volleyball game and Hoai at an English class at the Gap. It was also in that English class that the teacher, a young lieutenant of the U.S. Army, bought me a pocket-sized French-English/English-French dictionary as a gift which I still kept after so many years. I eventually gave it to my daughter Nikki when she started French classes in high school after telling her about the story behind it and how it had helped me with my limited English skills at the time.

Compared with Guam, life at the Gap was certainly an improvement, but most noteworthy was the food. In Guam, meals were served in a tent by the U.S. Army, but at the Gap, they were prepared and served in dining facilities by a food service company. There were several dining facilities across Areas 4 and 6 to serve the refugees, so most of the time there were no long lines, except for when chicken was on the menu. However, the opposite was true when fish was on the menu; not only was there no line, but the dining facilities would be mostly empty and bare as well. The kitchen staff just sat around bored, since barely a soul would be coming. The phenomenon appeared to be mindboggling for them, since for Americans, seafood was always considered more expensive than chicken. This could be easily explained though, because in Vietnam, chickens were not raised en mass like in the U.S., where much of the process is automated to allow a steady supply of cheap meat. In Vietnam, chickens were raised in yards and in cages, so for the average Vietnamese family, chicken was considered a luxury item and only served during special occasions. Fish, on the other hand, was more readily available and cheaper, since fishing was among the three major industries in Vietnam besides agriculture and forestry. So, whenever chicken was on the menu, everyone would tell each other to go early to avoid a long line.

One day while waiting in a long line (guess what was on the menu), a woman, who was near the front of the line, broke her water and gave birth to a baby. I was still not sure of what happened when I saw a woman wearing a white uniform came running out from the kitchen holding a knife in her hand, which she then used to cut the umbilical cord of the baby. It was an interesting scene to witness, when within minutes, there were at least half a dozen military vehicles that arrived at the scene to take the mother and the newborn baby to the Gap's General Hospital. The woman in the white uniform was a cook working in the dining hall; she heard the commotion outside and ran out to help; she was no doubt the unsung hero who saved the day.

Because of the spiritual need for some Buddhist refugees to have a place to pray, the theater in Area 6 was converted into a Buddhist temple. The service, however, was given in English by an American monk. One day, I saw a notice announcing the arrival of Rev. Thich Giac Duc, who would take over from the American monk. Giac Duc was a controversial figure who taught at Van Hanh University, the same university I attended in Saigon. Many people believed he was part of a Buddhist group that incited Buddhists and students to riot against the government and against the war. I decided to attend the "Meeting with Vietnamese Buddhist Refugees" organized by the people in charge of refugees' affair at the Gap to see what he was going to say.

The theater was jam-packed when I arrived, and Giac Duc was speaking at the lectern. As a Buddhist monk and university professor, Giac Duc was an excellent communicator and a skilled speaker, as I remembered him from the days at Van Hanh. Many people, especially young students, liked him for his unorthodox and straightforward speaking style. For example, when he advised us to learn English properly, he said we should read Times or Newsweek and not Playboy magazine. He knew how to rally people through passionate lectures about patriotism, thus when he criticized the antiwar songs by writer Trinh Cong Son during one of his lectures, he gave us the impression that he supported the war against the communists. But he also said it pained him as a Vietnamese to see the U.S. bomb North Vietnam and kill many Vietnamese civilians during its brutal bombing campaigns.

On that day in the theater at the Gap, he invited a guest speaker, an American Buddhist, to speak about how Vietnamese refugees could become a strong and united voice to help promote Buddhism in America. At the end of his lecture, Giac Duc asked if anyone had any questions for the guest speaker. A young Vietnamese man asked him whether what he said was realistic, since as refugees freshly arriving to America, our priority would be to find jobs to build new lives, and starting a Buddhist movement would be the last thing on our minds. The American speaker replied,

"2,500 years ago, there was only one man ..."

He was interrupted by applause across the room. Undeterred, the young Vietnamese retorted,

"We are not Buddha, we are not God, we are just ordinary people trying to start new lives here in a new country."

Giac Duc had to cut in and stopped the discussion. It was an interesting meeting. Years later, I saw Giac Duc again at the Buddhist Temple Giac Hoang in Washington, D.C., where he was preaching every Sunday. Eventually, I heard he got married and left the area to create a new Buddhist religious sect in Boston, Massachusetts that would allow clerical marriage like the Bhikkhu in Japan.

Summer passed, and with the cold weather fast approaching, we were still waiting for a sponsor. The fisherman and his family had already left, and the Catholic priest and his two disciples were also sponsored by the U.S. Catholic Church (USCC). The American Red Cross and the authorities who ran the refugee's settlement program had set a goal to have over 30,000 refugees moved out before the cold weather arrived. They worked and coordinated with religious and private organizations to find sponsors for the refugees quickly, but the priority was given to people with families. Tin came to us and asked if he could join "our family," and we thought it was a great idea since it would improve our chance of getting a sponsor, as the size of our family would be bigger. Hoai was also waiting for a sponsor with a group of his veteran buddies.

Then in October, when Falls arrived with cold winds blowing and leaves were changing to their vibrant colors, a Lutheran Church in Robesonia, Pennsylvania, had filed the paperwork to sponsor us. The authorities at the Gap informed us we would leave soon. Hoai and his friends also received the news that they would be sponsored by a different Lutheran Church from a nearby county.

On the big day, I remember it was a beautiful and cold Saturday morning; we were waiting at the rendez-vous place in Area 6 when our sponsors arrived in two large American cars to pick us up. We stopped at a restaurant by the highway to have lunch and then our sponsors took us to our new "home" which was a trailer in Wernersville, a small town about 60 miles east of Harrisburg. The trailer was in an area called Valley View Trailer Park off of Route 422. At the top of the hill was an old motel with a neon sign that said "Motel Deska". The person in charge of the program sponsoring us was a man named Joe C. He was a kind gentleman in his mid-forties, and visually impaired; he could only read up close. Joe and his wife, Barbara, took us to the supermarket to buy groceries and said that they would come to pick us up the next day to introduce us to the pastor and everyone at the church.

On Sunday, as promised, Joe and Barbara came by the trailer to take us to church. We also met their two teenage children, Karen and Bryan. At the church, we felt a little uneasy to be the stars of the show, as everyone's eyes focused on us. After all, we were three Vietnamese guys from a place faraway that people only knew about from the name of the war. When the choir was singing, I noticed a girl who kept staring at me, and at the end of the mass as the group was going down the aisles while still singing, she stopped at the row where we were sitting with Joe's family and held out her hand toward me. While I still did not understand what was going on, Joe turned and winked at me, saying, "She wants you to hold her hand." I took her hand, and I noticed everyone was holding each other's hand to walk around the aisles and sing the last gospel song. That was the first time I attended a mass at any church, let alone an American church.

After the mass, Joe introduced us to Victor K., the pastor of the church, who was a very amicable man. Joe told us the church had found jobs for all three of us and we would start our jobs on Monday. He explained further that I would work for a flag company in Womelsdorf, my brother would work for a kitchen cabinet company in Robesonia, and Tin would work for Chit Chat Farm, a rehabilitation place for addicts in Wernersville. The church had also arranged transportation for all of us. We were thankful for everything Joe and his church did for us, and we realized that the reason it took a while for us to get sponsored was because Joe wanted to work out all the details before he could get us out of the Gap.

In 1975, Wernersville had a population of about 2,000. The entire town had one post office, one bank, and one super market just like in the lesson about a small town in America from the "English for Today" book I learned in Saigon. We were told that a member of the church was especially kind to let us use his trailer for free and that we only had to pay for the utilities once we got our first paychecks. After a few months, as we were adjusting to our new life, the winter arrived, and we got our first taste of the cold weather here in this northeast state. Every morning when it was still dark, we walked up to the top of the hill near the Motel Deska sign to wait for our rides in the bitterly cold weather. It was at those moments that I noticed the motel looked kind of creepy. It always looked old and deserted and reminded me of the Bates Motel, in which I imagined Anthony Perkins would appear out of nowhere dressed in his mother's dress, holding a big long knife, and chase us around in the snow.

Every Saturday, Barbara and Joe would pick us up to go to the supermarket to buy food for the week and then again on Sunday to go to church. Because of his poor vision, Joe did not drive, so it was Barbara who drove us around until we bought our own cars the next summer. Although none of us were Christian, we enjoyed going to church, as everyone was super nice and we did not experience any prejudice toward us. After the morning mass, we would stay to study English with members of the church who had volunteered to teach us the language. My "teacher" was Donna, the 17-year-old girl with blond hair and brown eyes from the church choir, whom I met the first time at the church. Every

Sunday afternoon during our English class, we would lie down on the floor next to each other in the Bible classroom and we would just talk and she would correct my pronunciation whenever I said something incorrect. I told her about the city called Saigon where I was born and what it was like growing up there during the war. She was surprised that I knew quite a bit about the American culture, especially the Rock & Roll music and Woodstock.

During the week, I worked at the Valley Forge Flag Company. I found out that the company was a historical flag company dating back to when its founded in 1882. Today, it is still the leading flag supplier to the U.S. government. The flags made by the company have been flown by the U.S. Armed Forces in so many wars and conflicts, including the Vietnam War. In 1975, it was ironic for me to work for the company that made the U.S. flags that were not only flown in my home country during the war, but perhaps even used to cover caskets of U.S. soldiers who died protecting the freedom and democracy there.

On my first day of work, the manager, who was a small lady with white hair named Sarah, took me on a tour to show me around the plant. When she came in front of a door with the sign "Men," she paused to tell me this was the men's room and that it was for me to use. Then, as soon as she finished talking, the door opened, and a lady walked out. We all shared a good laugh. I understood later why Sarah was trying to tell me about the men's room; since all the employees at the flag factory were female, the ladies had been using the men's room as an extra bathroom. There was a middle-aged man I saw who came around once in a while to repair or do maintenance on the sewing machines, but otherwise, I was the only male employee there. As such, I felt I always received special treatment from the female workers there, especially those I worked directly with.

My job was to pick up and fold the flags after they were sewn together by the sewing machine operators and put them in the boxes. Thus, I had the chance to talk to my female coworkers every day and received tons of motherly advice from those wonderful ladies at the factory. The ladies also took turns to invite me to their houses for dinners and lunches. One lady in particular, named Debbie, tried to teach me how to drive on her stick shift Volkswagen. After I almost drove her car into a ditch near her house because I had problem handling the clutch and the gas pedal, she quit teaching me how to drive. I ended up getting driving lessons from YMCA in Reading where Joe had signed up for all of us there. Our driving instructor was a guy from Puerto Rico. He was a married man, but that did not stop him from having fun. During our lessons, he would drive us around the city and honk at every pretty girl we passed by in the streets, and they would wave back at us smiling. After each lesson, he would take us to his home and his wife made us fried rice with pork chops to eat.

One day, a guy from church took us to the slopes of South Mountain in Wernersville to show off his car. It was a 1968 Mustang with a rebuilt V-8 engine that pumped out over 360 horsepower. He asked us to get in for a ride; he said he was going to take us for a spin in his car. Little did we know he was about to give us a fright in our lives. As soon as he floored the gas pedal, I knew we were in trouble. He was driving up and down the slopes as fast as he could, while maintaining control of the car with his brake, making loud screeching noises as the tires scrubbed against the road's surface. I felt dizzy and gripped my seat the entire time. When the car stopped, I almost threw up while he just looked at us with a big grin on his face. Although I was frightened, I had to admit he was a skillful driver, but I would not get in his car ever again.

The first time I saw the snow was during one early morning at the factory. I watched it falling through the giant windows of the old red brick building where we worked. The sky was still dark, and the snow looked like big white cotton balls falling from the sky, landing on the tree branches, the windows, and on the ground under the ambient of the street lamps, creating a beautiful picture like a canvas painting. All the ladies working on the floor rushed to my side and pointed to the snow. They appeared to be more excited than I was. Some gave me advice on how to drive in the snow, although I did not even own a car at the time.

When summer came, we had saved enough money to buy our first cars -used cars, that is-, so that we did not have to rely on others for transportation. My brother bought a big 1970 Pontiac Lemans, Tin bought a 1971 Volkswagen Beetle, and as for me, I bought a red hot 1970 2-door Ford Maverick with a manual stick shift. It was probably a mistake for me, not because of anything wrong with the car, but because of the manual transmission. The trailer park had a lot of steep slopes, so getting in and out of street side parking was challenging if your car was in between two cars. Nevertheless, having our own cars was a big step for all of us. Barbara would not have to take us grocery shopping every weekend anymore, and most importantly, we could commute to work independently.

After buying the car, I often drove along the long back roads to practice my driving skill while enjoying the open countryside. I usually rolled down the windows and let the wind blow freely on my hair and face. For the first time in a long while, I felt so peaceful. I would turn on the radio, and I would drive like that for hours without the need to know where I was going.

One afternoon, I drove up to Debbie's house, which was up on a hill in the countryside near Womelsdorf. She had invited me over for lunch with her and her daughter Susan. On the way back near a major highway intersection, I ran into a dense fog with zero visibility. I could see nothing at all in front of the car. I did not know what to do, so I stopped near the middle of the intersection and just sat in the car and waited. But the fog was getting thicker, and I was afraid I would be a sitting duck if another car or truck came from behind and hit my car. I finally drove forward across the intersection while pressing on the car horn repeatedly until I passed the dense fog area. It was as a frightening experience, as if I was blindfolded while crossing the street at the same time.

After we got home from work one day, two young boys knocked on our door and said they wanted to be friends and hang out with us. Michael had long brown hair and looked a lot like the young James Taylor, and Johnny was somewhat chubby with curly and dirty blond hair. They were both about the same age, thirteen or fourteen. They usually brought with them things like old records of the Beatles to show us, although we did not have a record player. One time they brought a kitten and wanted us to have it, and I named her "Zipper" because she ran pretty fast. Another time they brought some joints and wanted us to smoke with them. We had the feeling that they wanted to show off or impress us, but otherwise they were good kids and we were glad they felt comfortable being friends with us as we also enjoyed their company.

For a time, life seemed to be good, although we still got homesick every once in a while, especially when something triggered our memories or reminded us of home. We were happy with our jobs and everything, but we knew something was missing - something we could not find here in this small town, and we wanted to explore other opportunities outside of Wernersville. After all, the U.S. is a big country.

I knew I wanted to go back to college and Tin said he would follow us wherever we go. My brother Thang decided to go to Washington, D.C. to find out if there were better opportunities in the capital region, and we would join him later. He was able to contact our cousin Thao, who was living in Takoma Park, Maryland, so he would stay at her place until he could find a job. Thao worked for the Department of Interior of the Republic of South Vietnam and was training in the U.S. when Saigon fell. She found a sponsor and was taking some classes at a community college in Takoma Park. In the meantime, Tin and I would continue to stay in Pennsylvania for a while, at least until my brother settled down.

After my brother left for D.C., Hoai called and asked to stay with us. His army buddy had moved to another state, and he did not want to live by himself. I told him, "Of course." We did not know when we would move to Washington, D.C., but it was good to have Hoai with us in the meantime.

Time went by fast. The cold weather signaled the change of season, and soon, the Thanksgiving holiday was approaching. I remember our first Thanksgiving when we just got out of the Gap, Joe and Barbara invited all of us to their house for Thanksgiving dinner with their family. It was our first experience of having a traditional American Thanksgiving dinner with our sponsor's family. It was a pleasant evening. After dinner, we took a walk to the town center to see the Christmas trees for sale there. I remember the temperature was freezing cold that night, and Joe asked me if I was cold, but I put on a brave face and said not really, although I was trembling. The next day, Joe and Barbara took us to go shopping for our winter coats.

When Thanksgiving came the next year, we celebrated it at our trailer. The day after Thanksgiving, Hoai and Tin had to work but the flag company was closed, thus I got to stay home and was planning to enjoy a long four-day weekend. When Hoai and Tin got home from work that Friday, Tin said he wanted to go and grab some beers, while Hoai wanted to go to the bank to add his wife and child as beneficiaries to his account in case something happened to him. At the time, I did not pay any attention to this or ask him why.

Hoai said he would drive, so we all went inside his car. He had a Volkswagen Beetle like the one Tin had, but his car was green while Tin's was orange. I climbed into the back seat of Hoai's two-door Beetle and Tin sat in the front passenger seat. Then, for some unknown reason, I changed mind and decided to stay home instead to get dinner ready. And so, I climbed out of the car.

Around 6:00 PM, while I was preparing for dinner, I heard a series of siren sounds from atop the highway. It continued for a while, and then I heard a knock on the door. I opened it, and it was the neighbor who lived in the trailer next to us.

"I think your friends were involved in a car accident."

"Really? Are they ok?"

"I think you'd better go see."

I put on my winter coat and ran up the hill. It was already dark and cold outside; I turned the collar of my coat up to keep warm. When I got to the top of the hill near the Motel Deska sign, my eyes were dazzled by the flashes of all kinds of different lights from the police cars, ambulance, and fire trucks. It took me a while to realize what was going on, and then immediately I saw Hoai's Volkswagen, or rather what was left of it, in the middle of the highway. The front of the car was almost obliterated as it had crumbled into the front seats and the rear of the car was also unrecognizable. "Oh my God!" I said to myself. There was debris everywhere, and a large crowd of spectators had gathered around the perimeter that the police had set up with road flares. There were police officers and emergency personnel walking back and forth at the scene.

I looked around and that was when I saw a body laying nearby the side of the highway. Although it was covered with a blanket, I recognized Hoai's green army jacket sticking out from underneath. I felt my heart skip a beat, and as I tried to go near him, a state police officer stopped me.

"Sir, you cannot go there."

"But he is my friend."

"I understand, but you should not go there."

"What happened to my other friend? Where is he? Is he ok?"

"They took him to the hospital. He received severe head injuries and is in critical condition. I am sorry."

I saw Mark, a member of the Lutheran Church, who also worked as a volunteer with the Berk County Fire & Rescue Department. He came over to talk to me, but I did not hear a word of what he said, as I was in shock and numb with what happened. I told him I wanted to go to the hospital to see Tin, but he said that the police had blocked the highway in both directions and that I would not be able to get through.

I went back to the trailer and called Joe to let him and Barbara know what happened. After the highway was cleared, Joe and Barbara came by and we all went to Reading Hospital Center together. We met with the ER doctor who told us that Tin received severe head and internal injuries and that his prognosis was not very good. I asked the doctor:

"Can I see him?"

"I would not recommend it. It's not a pretty sight."

"It's ok. He is my friend."

"Are you sure?"

"Yes."

The doctor took me to a room in the ICU area and I saw Tin lying there, unconscious with his eyes closed and with some kind of device inserted into his throat to keep him breathing. The doctor said he would call me later if there were any changes to Tin's condition and recommended that I go home to rest. Joe and Barbara suggested I should stay at their place for the night, but I insisted on going back to the trailer.

Later that night, the doctor called me and said Tin was "brain dead" and he passed during the night after they disconnected the breathing tube. Although I already knew, I was still shocked. I looked around the trailer and imagined the voices and laughs of the friends with whom I had shared the space over the past months. I wondered how ironic for Hoai and Tin to escape the war and the harrowing journey to come to America and only to die in a car accident caused by a drunk driver.

I could not help but wonder whether it was fate or destiny as to why I decided to get out of Hoai's car at the last minute. Would I have also died in the crash if I stayed in the car? Or would that have changed what had happened, and my friends would still be alive? Was it simply not my time to go? Was it fate that put Lloyd M. Gerhart, the driver of the car that caused the accident, at the exact moment on Route 422 with Hoai and Tin? And why did Hoai want to add his wife and child as beneficiaries to his bank account - did he know or feel that something was going to happen to him, or was it just pure coincidence? If he did not stop by the bank, the timing would have changed and maybe the accident would not have happened. Was it fate or destiny? Or was it a guardian angel who was watching over me? I kept asking myself those questions over and over.

According to the police report, Hoai's Volkswagen
Beetle was halted in the middle/passing lane near Valley
View Trailer Park when it was struck in the back by a
sedan driven by Gerhart. The impact pushed the compact
sedan into the westbound lane and path of a pickup truck
driven by Jerry Witwer. The Volkswagen was crunched
between Gerhart's sedan and Witwer's pickup. Both
Hoai and Tin were thrown from the vehicle; Hoai was
lying on the north berm about 25 feet from the car and
Tin was found on the highway several feet from the
wreckage. The Township Police Chief said Hoai's auto
was waiting to make a left turn into the trailer park and
the car turn signals were on at the time. Gerhart was
charged with involuntary manslaughter and drunken
driving. Hoai and Tin became the county's 59th and 60th
traffic fatalities of the year.

According to the U.S. Government statistics, in 1976,
there were 45,523 traffic deaths in the U.S. The number
of traffic fatalities has since decreased significantly due to
better and safer vehicle designs, with seat belts and airbags
being credited with savings thousands of lives, as well as
increases in enforcement of tougher laws and greater
public awareness of the dangers of drinking and driving.
Still, more than 38,000 people die every year in crashes
on U.S. roadways, in which alcohol-related crashes
account for much of these traffic fatalities.

In January 2017, my brother Thang, Michelle, and I
returned to Pennsylvania to attend a memorial service for
Joe, who had passed away at 81, and saw Barbara, Karen,
Bryan, and some of the other people at the church who
had helped us when we first came to the U.S. The
memorial service to honor Joe's life was held at the Christ

Church United Church of Christ in Elizabethtown, Pennsylvania. Apparently, Joe and Barbara had moved back to Elizabethtown from Robesonia years ago. Elizabethtown was where Joe went to college and where he and Barbara met in 1958. Joe was more than a sponsor to us; he was also a friend and a father figure, and we really missed him. The first time Joe introduced us to the hamburger was during a trip to McDonald's; he said hotdogs used to be American's favorite delicacies but in the 70s, hamburgers had taken over the first place. Nonetheless, both hotdogs and hamburgers are as American as apple pie and baseball. During the entire time I worked at the flag factory, I had a hotdog for lunch from a lunch truck that came around noon every day. I felt I was learning to be American, and eating hotdogs and drinking coca-cola seemed to be cool and American.

We also went to visit Hoai and Tin in Myerstown. The memorial park was empty and somewhat gloomy on a sad winter afternoon. We felt an air of melancholy surround us as we looked at the two grave markers laid side by side on the ground. We felt solace in knowing that our friends had each other throughout all these years and hoped that they had finally found eternal peace.

Duy Tan Street; Our apartment building was at the end of the street, in the opposite direction of the Notre Dame Cathedral of Saigon. *(Source by manhhai via Flickr)*

The first T-54 tank crashed through the Independent Palace's gates on April 30, 1975. This was one of the tanks we saw on our way to the Navy Yard.
(Source: CBS News)

This government building was across the street from the U.S. Embassy. *(Source by manhhai via Flickr)*

A column of smoke arising from Tan Son Nhut Air Base in the evening of April 28, 1975. *(Source by manhhai via Flickr)*

HQ 402 on its way to the open ocean on May 1, 1975.
*(Courtesy of Cao The Hung via Bien Xua, biển xưa
(wordpress.com)*

HQ 402 off the cost of Da Nang rescuing SVN
Marines
in March 1975.
*(Courtesy of Cao The Hung via Bien Xua, biển xưa
(wordpress.com)*

Refugees from **HQ 402** were being transferred to **HQ 06**.
(Photo by James Bongaard, Source: NHHC VN Collection)

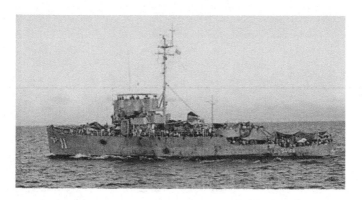

HQ 11 on its way to Subic Bay.
(Photo by Hugh Doyle. Source: NHHC VN Collection)

A flotilla of South Vietnamese Navy battleships escorted by
USS Kirk on the way to Subic Bay.
(Photo by Hugh Doyle. Source: NHHC VN Collection)

Ceremony to lower the flag of
the Republic of South
Vietnam on one of the SVN
battleships off the coast of the
Philippines.

*(Photo by Hugh Doyle.
Source: NHHC VN
Collection)*

Sign welcomes Vietnamese refugees on board USS Bayfield, Sept. 1954. *(Source: navytimes.com)*

We stayed at this "Tent City" in Guam, May – June 1975.

(Pinterest by Alexanne Stone)

Refugee Evacuation Card. *(Author's Collection)*

Refugee Medical
Screening Record.
(Author's Collection)

This dictionary was given to
me from a young lieutenant
of the U.S. Army at the Gap
in 1975. *(Author's
Collection)*

"The Gap"
(Source: Militay.com)

One of these barracks in
Area 6 was our home,
June–September 1975.
*(Source:
saigonocean.com)*

Valley Forge Flag Co. where I
worked 1975-76
(Do Family Archives)

Crumbled, twisted remains of Hoai's Volkswagen
(Photo by Clifford R. Yeich)

Hoai and Tin's graves in Myerstown, PA
(Author's Collection)

(L-R) Joe, Thang, Barbara, me, Michelle and Nikki visiting Hoai and Tin in Myerstown, PA.
(Do Family Archives)

Joe and Barbara Cook
(Courtesy of Barbara Cook)

(L-R) Michelle, me and Joe in 1993.
(Courtesy of Barbara C.)

(L-R) Thang, Barabara and Joe in 1993.
(Courtesy of Barbara Cook)

REUNIFICATION

In December 1976, after the funerals of Hoai and Tin, I moved to the Washington, D.C. area to rejoin my brother, Thang. I registered to go to a community college in Takoma Park and tried to restart my life. The D.C. metropolitan area includes parts of Maryland and Virginia, and had a small Vietnamese community. I was glad to meet some compatriots on campus. My brother and I moved in with a group of friends to share the rent. I applied and received federal grants to help pay for part of my tuition, and worked on a work-study program during the week. To help pay for living expenses, I also worked at a Japanese restaurant in Georgetown on the weekends.

I also drank with a group of friends. First, we only drank on the weekends, then we drank whenever we got together, perhaps because of boredom and loneliness. During the weekends, after I got off from work at the restaurant, I usually went out to drink until past midnight. One time while I was driving home, I was so drunk that every time I opened my eyes; I found myself on the opposite side of the road. It was a miracle that I made it home without getting myself or someone killed or being stopped by the police. My guardian angel must have been watching over me again! When I made it to the front door, I totally passed out. After that incident, I told myself I would never drink and drive again; I should have known better since I just lost two friends because of a drunk driver. However, my drinking problem continued, and it had affected my studies negatively; for almost three years from 1977 to 1979, I could not complete all credits required to either receive an AA degree or transfer to a four-year university. It seemed like my life was going in the wrong direction.

Meanwhile, at home in Saigon, my parents heard rumors that the Navy ship we were on had gone down in the ocean and everyone onboard had died, but the information was vague, in which there was no way to confirm. Desperately wanting to find out about our status, my mother went to see a fortune teller who told her that my brother and I had died. My mother was devastated. According to my sister Mai, she cried for days, but still the family could tell no one. My parents were afraid if the communists found out that they had two sons who escaped (and died!), they would send our entire family to the "new economic zone." Life under communist rule was harsh; you could trust no one, even your neighbors.

After the fall of Saigon, the communist government implemented a cruel and vindictive policy to treat former officers, employees of the South Vietnamese government, religious leaders, intellectuals and their families, including people who worked for or had any connections with the

U.S. government. It was a systematic approach similar to the one used by the Nazis. First, they sent the men to the so-called "re-education camps" in remote areas, mostly near the western and northern borders. "Re-education Camp" was a fancy name for forced labor camp as part of their indoctrination and forced confession program. They claimed the camps were places where people could redeem themselves by learning about the lenient policy of the communist party, and abandoning any anti-revolutionary thoughts before they could re-enter the society. The men were told to pack enough clothes for several days, but in reality, many were kept for ten years or more. It was estimated that between 500,000 and one million people were sent to these camps; many endured torture, starvation, and disease, and many did not survive the ordeal.

In the next phase, the communist government seized the homes of the people they had sent to the "re-education camps" by forcing their family members to go to the "new economic zones," which were described as uninhabited mountainous or forested areas. They were told to farm and build their own places to live with no help from the government. According to French journalist Jean Lacouture, who visited a new economic zone in 1976, "it was a prefabricated hell and a place one goes to only if the alternative to it would be death." It was estimated that between 1975 and 1980, over one million people were forced to move to these new economic zones.

Our family was lucky to stay at the Duy Tan apartment complex because the communist government still needed my father to work at the Vietnam National

Bank to train new employees who were coming from the North. After the communist forces took over Saigon on April 30, 1975, the communist provisional government moved quickly to take control of the Vietnam National Bank, which was the central repository of the national financial assets, including sixteen tons of gold bullion stored securely in the bank vault, that, according to several false rumors, were taken out of the country by President Thieu.

On September 22, 1975, the communist government implemented the first wave of a "money exchange" policy. They claimed that the goal was to erase social inequalities between the rich and poor people. Each family was allowed to exchange only up to $100,000 dong of the old currency to $200 new dong. The exchange rate was $500 old dong for $1 new dong. Anything over $100,000 dong would belong to the government. My father was asked to report to a local branch with other employees to support the money exchange operation. When people learned of the impending operation, they went out to buy and spend as much as possible since after the exchange, the old currency would become useless and hold no monetary value even if you intended to hide the monies.

On March 5, 1978, in an effort to move the country further to socialism/communism, the communist politburo implemented another money exchange policy to erase private commercial enterprises and build cooperatives. For people living in the city, the policy allowed one person living alone to exchange $100 dong, $200 dong for a family of two and $50 dong for each additional person after that, but the maximum amount could not exceed $500 dong. For the people living in the countryside, $100 dong could be exchanged for every family of two, and for a family of more than two, each additional person was allowed to exchange $30, in which the maximum exchange amount allowed was $300 dong. Any amount in excess of the limits had to be reported and deposited into government-controlled bank accounts. The money could only be withdrawn for valid reasons. Additionally, the account owners had to prove that the money in their accounts was their own hard-earned monies.

By this time, my father no longer worked for the bank. He had been forced to retire and terminated by the communist government because they no longer needed his service. As such, our family had no money left to exchange. My sister Mai later told me that between 1978 and 1979, our family was in a precarious situation with nothing to eat. They survived only by borrowing money and food from others. Most people survived by eating "bo bo" rice called sorghum, a type of grain used to feed livestock.

In December 1978, Vietnam invaded Cambodia and overthrew the Khmer Rouge government of Pol Pot who was responsible for the genocide of two million of its people. Pol Pot and the Khmer Rouge then waged a guerrilla war against Vietnam, in which both China and the U.S. provided military aid to Pol Pot, while the Soviet Union supported the Vietnamese. Despite receiving generous support from China and the U.S., the Khmer Rouge could not withstand the Vietnamese offensive and suffered heavy casualties. China eventually intervened and launched cross-border attacks on the northern part of

Vietnam. After 27 days, China withdrew its troop from Vietnam after failing to force a Vietnamese withdrawal from Cambodia. In retaliation, Vietnam expelled hundreds of thousands of ethnic Chinese from Vietnam. Vietnamese troops remained in Cambodia for a decade. During this period, Cambodia was run virtually as a Vietnamese colony, until September 1989, when the last Vietnamese troops left Cambodia.

The wars with Cambodia and China exacted heavy human casualties for Vietnam. My younger brother Dai would have been called to serve in those wars if not for my mother, who reached out to her old friend for help. When my mother fled the communists back in 1954, and migrated to the South with her family, her friend stayed in the North. She later joined the communist party and eventually became a high-ranking member who had some power to get my brother off the draft list. At first, she was reluctant, since our parents were listed as "people of the old regime" who had very little rights in the new society. However, out of old friendship, she agreed to help. It was the extent to which she would do as a favor for my mother.

The economic hardship and wars forced many people, including tens of thousands of ethnic Chinese, to flee Vietnam. Although people had been fleeing the country by boat and ship following the end of the war in 1975, the real mass exodus occurred in 1978 and 1979. But in order to leave the country, you would have needed money or gold to bribe communist officials to get exit permits, documentation, and a ship or boat usually in poor condition, all of which would cost around $3,000 in gold bars for an adult and half of that for a child. It was a large sum that often only the well-to-do could afford. Even for the poorer Vietnamese, who wanted to leave secretly without documentation, usually in the dark of night, would have had to pay the smugglers or boat owners substantial fares to have a place in the tiny and flimsy boats. Even so, thousands of people continued to leave in small boats despite enormous dangers at sea, such as storms, diseases, starvation and pirates. It was estimated that between 1975 and 1995, the number of people who left Vietnam by boat and arrived safely in other countries totaled around 800,000. There are no official numbers of those who did not make it, but the rough estimate by the United Nations High Commission for Refugees was that between 200,000 and 400,000 people died at sea.

By 1979, the situation reached a humanitarian crisis level, in which the United Nations had to convene an international conference in Geneva to discuss the issue. As a result of the conference, Vietnam agreed to allow orderly departures of Vietnamese people for resettlements to other countries, so that people would not have to leave by boat. The South East Asian countries agreed to let refugees stay temporarily while waiting for resettlement, and the Western countries agreed to accelerate resettlement. The agreement became known as the Orderly Departure Program, or ODP.

Until 1979, we had not contacted home to let our parents know we were okay for fear that it might cause them trouble with the communists. But by the end of 1979, we felt an urgency to write home. At the time, the U.S. did not have a diplomatic relationship with Vietnam, so a direct letter from us with an U.S. postal address would have been too risky. Therefore, my brother Thang decided to send a letter through our uncle in France using an alias that started with the initial of each of his names. Mai told us that one morning in December 1979, she heard the mailman shouting from the main level of the Duy Tan building that Apartment 26 had mail, so she ran down from the third floor to receive the letter. At first, she did not know it was from my brother, she just saw that it was from a "Dang Quoc Thai" with a return address in Paris, France. Then she showed it to my parents and when they opened and read it, they knew. They knew it was from us and that we were alive and well. It took several months for us to receive a letter back from them since it had to take a detour through France, but we were glad that finally, we were able to make contact with our family.

The letter was a desperate cry for help to send anything we could: food, money, medicine, as our family was in dire need of assistance. We went out to the store and bought everything we could think of, and we even rolled a hundred-dollar bill and stuck it inside a toothpaste tube after carefully marking it. We packed everything into a large box and sent it back directly to the Duy Tan address. There was no time to waste. The letter from home was also a wake-up call for me. I quit drinking and stayed sober for good.

In 1980, I transferred to a private technical college with the goal of getting my Bachelor's degree in electronics engineering in two years, and find a job so I would be better able to help my brother and my family in Vietnam. To pay for the tuition, I applied for student loans. I knew that this time; I needed to focus on my studies just like that time in Saigon when I studied for my baccalaureate exam.

In the meantime, my brother continued to send "gift boxes" home regularly to help our family. With our help, our family could breathe a little easier; my mother would bring the items we sent home and resell them at the open market for cash to buy food and other necessities. We also tried to find a way to send money directly to them more quickly, but since the U.S. did not have a normal relationship with Vietnam, it was tricky to do so without running afoul of the law. A friend told me he knew someone who could transfer the money to Vietnam for us. The way it works, he explained, was that we would give the money to that person, and she would contact her people in Saigon, who would go to the apartment and give the money in Vietnamese currency at the agreed upon exchange rate to my parents.

We decided to give it a try, and it worked out well for a while, until one day there was a knock on our door at the apartment where we lived in Gaithersburg, Maryland. When I answered the door, a man in a business suit showed me a badge and identified himself as an FBI agent, and wanted to come in to talk to us. He said we had nothing to worry about, he just wanted to ask some questions. After I invited him in, he explained the FBI had been investigating a woman who took money from people in the U.S. with the purpose of sending it to their families in Vietnam, but she never gave the money to them. He said the woman took the money and disappeared. He asked,

"Have you ever given money to a woman or anyone to have them sent it to your family in Vietnam?"

"We did, in fact, give money to a mutual friend, but we never met the person who handled the transaction," I replied nervously.

"Did you know if the person was a woman or a man?"

"I am not sure, but I think it was a woman."

"Did you know if your family in Vietnam received the money?"

"Yes"

"I would be careful if I were you. You could lose your money."

The FBI agent gave me his business card before he left and said to call him if I came across any information about the woman. I never asked the agent how he got my name and my address, as I was afraid it would lead to more questions from him about my friend. I did not want to get him into trouble with the FBI. Consequently, we stopped sending money through the woman, and instead, we would send more "gift boxes" home.

In 1980, with our support, my parents gathered everything the family owned to buy enough gold bars to secure a place on a boat for my 16-year-old brother Cuong. The organizer, however, took the money, and turned everyone over to the communists. The communists arrested everyone who was supposed to go on the boat. Because he was a minor, Cuong was eventually released after spending 6 months in jail.

Also in 1980, we were eligible to apply for our U.S. citizenship since we had been in the U.S. for five years as permanent residents. My brother went ahead and filed for the application, while I wanted to wait because I was busy with my course load and needed to save money for the application fee. After my brother got his U.S. citizenship, he began the process of filing a petition for our family to come to the U.S.

The year of 1982 seemed to be a miracle year for us. Everything that happened, happened in a good and peculiar way, as if planned by God. In May, I graduated six months earlier than planned. I had also applied for U.S. citizenship and became a U.S. citizen shortly before I graduated from college. The huge military spending during the Reagan administration had helped boost the job market in the defense industry area, and I had no problem getting a job as an electrical engineer with a defense company in Virginia. Becoming a U.S. citizen had certainly helped me get the job and obtain the necessary security clearance.

On the day I was scheduled for the Naturalization Oath Ceremony to become a U.S. citizen, Joe and Barbara drove from Pennsylvania to Maryland to attend the naturalization ceremony with me. Joe said it was a very special event, and unless you are an immigrant, you would never get to experience it, for it is a privilege and an honor to be a U.S. citizen, something that too many people who were born in this country take for granted.

My brother was also notified by the Immigration and Naturalization Service (INS) that his petition was approved, and soon we would be reunited with our family. In Saigon, my parents were also notified by the U.S. consulate to apply for immigrant visas for the entire family. After that, it was just a matter of waiting for an interview with a consulate officer, undergoing medical examinations, and getting certain vaccinations before the visas could be issued. My brother also received a request from the National Visa Center (NVC) to submit various financial and supporting documents to make sure we would be responsible for our family once they were in the U.S. It was perfect timing, since by then, I already had a full-time job, and between my brother and me, we could support our family financially. To prepare for their arrival, we moved from our one-bedroom apartment in Gaithersburg to a townhouse we rented in Rockville. And finally in July, we received a letter from our parents stating their visas had been approved, and the next thing we knew, they were in Bangkok, Thailand, waiting for the next flight to Washington, D.C.

The international flight arrived in Washington, D.C. late in the evening, after making a stop in New York City. My brother, our cousin Thao, and I were waiting for our family at the gate. When we saw them, we could not hold back our tears. It was approximately seven years and three months since the day we left Saigon and last saw them. It was surreal, and I had thought that this day would never come.

When I first saw my family again, I noticed that something was not right with my sister Thu. I asked my mother, and only then did she tell me that after we left in 1975, Thu became withdrawn, and began having problems keeping up with school. A school official called my mother one day and said that Thu could not follow instructions, and could not keep up with her classmates, so the school had no choice but to send her home. My mother took her to see a doctor, who diagnosed her with schizophrenia.

As it happened, her illness almost cost her the visa to the U.S.; Mai said that on the day of departure, while the whole family was at the airport, an immigration official said Thu could not travel to the U.S. with the rest of the family because she did not have the proper approval based on her medical record. My mother thought that she would have to stay back with Thu. Then at the last minute, as the family was about to board the plane, a miracle happened: a person from the U.S. Consulate ran out to the gate with the signed documentation, and said Thu could leave with the family. I was dismayed at the suspense our family had to go through, and was glad that Thu and our mother could come with the family.

Years later, when I discussed the miracle with my sisters Mai and Anh, we learned it was not really a miracle after all. We believed it was actually the communist officials at the airport who did not want to let Thu go unless our family pay them. It was customary for communist officials to expect money included with the paperwork otherwise, they would delay or make life difficult for people leaving or entering the country. I heard stories about people putting money inside their passports when they went through customs upon arriving, usually something like a twenty-dollar bill. We think they would want a lot more money when people were trying to leave, especially in Thu's situation, but my mother would not budge and refused to pay them. So, at the last minute, they had to let Thu go with the rest of the family.

When we left Saigon in 1975, our youngest sister, Anh, was only seven. We did not realize how quick our brothers and sisters had grown up in seven years. With our family finally together again, Thang went back to school and earned a bachelor's degree in electrical engineering, and also a master's degree in computer science. And I took on the role of supporting our family, so my brothers and sisters could all have a chance to go to college. I told them to succeed in America; they need to work hard but it would be helpful to have a college degree. I also went back to school to pursue my master's degree in engineering while working full time.

As our family was settling down and adjusting to changes in a new country, we also experienced family problems because of different personalities and conflicts. But all families have problems and no family is perfect. Leo Tolstoy wrote in the opening paragraph in his book Anna Karenina: "All happy families are alike; each unhappy family is unhappy in its own way", and our family was no different. My mother had to play the role of a peacemaker to keep our family together. During this period, I was dating around and was seldom home. My mother was not all too happy. She said she would like for me to settle down and get married to a nice girl.

A mechanical engineer named Kevin at the company I worked, told me one day, he wanted me to meet a friend of his, a nice and pretty young woman, he said. At the time, I was in a relationship with another person, so I kept pushing him off. However, I did not want to turn down the invitation since I was trying to get out of a relationship that both parties agreed that would go nowhere, but neither of us knew how to break up without hurting the other. Despite Kevin's good intention, I could not work out a date which would be mutually good for me and the "mystery" young woman whom Kevin kept praising. When I left the company to accept an offer with another firm, I did not pursue the matter further.

About a year later, our cousin Thao told me her friend, Loan, who used to work with her at the Interior Department in Saigon, had a young and pretty sister named Michelle, and perhaps I wanted to meet her. By this time, my previous relationship had ended, albeit amicably, and I was not seeing anyone in particular, so I agreed. However, I could not keep the appointment because of an unexpected event at the last minute, and had to reschedule the meeting. Our next date also had to be rescheduled, because Michelle had a conflict. The third time was a charm, and I finally met Michelle at our cousin Thao's place. We clicked with each other right away; we talked about jobs, families, hobbies, among others. She was excited about starting her new job the next Monday. As she was talking about her new job, she mentioned a friend from her previous job who had tried to set her up with someone. The guy, she said, was arrogant, who repeatedly pushed off meeting with her. She was glad it did not work out with him. Feeling suspicious, I immediately asked her,

"Was your friend's name Kevin?"

"Yes! How do you know?"

It turned out Michelle was the "mystery" date I kept missing a year ago. We both laughed off and thought it was such a rare and remarkable coincidence. I told her it must be fate that brought us together, as we could not escape from each other. A year later, we were married.

By the late eighties, the worst of the international humanitarian crisis involving the Vietnamese boat people was over, although people were still leaving the country and thousands still died at sea. In 1987, I just completed my graduate degree at George Mason University in

Virginia, and worked for a big defense contractor in
Washington, D.C. A colleague at the company told me,

"The U.S. should not accept any more refugees.
These boat people are not political refugees, they are
economic refugees."

The colleague was an Italian American who had just
recently become a naturalized U.S. citizen himself. As a
Vietnamese refugee, the boat people crisis was personal
to me; my family could be among those people. Many of
my friends had escaped by boats, many lost members of
their families. A woman I know lost both of her parents
and her sister. She and her two young sons survived the
journey and the Thai pirates. Her husband was in a "re-
education camp" in a remote area in North Vietnam. So,
I told him,

"You don't have a clue about what these people have
gone through. Do you know that according to the United
Nations High Commission for Refugees, hundreds of
thousands of the boat people died at sea? The estimates
are that up to seventy percent died at sea. Would you
take your family to go on a journey solely for economic
reasons when you know the odds are against you, and that
all of you could die at sea?"

The Italian was silent for a moment and then he
said,

"But the U.S. cannot continue to accept more and
more people into the country. I have a daughter who is
young, and I am worried about her future."

I was appalled by his answer, but I had heard it
before. He was definitely not alone in that thinking,
especially with current sentiments about immigrants who
did not originate from European countries. Perhaps he

was a racist who believed in white privilege, or perhaps he was just ignorant, and was looking at the U.S. economy as an apple pie, in which the more people who came the smaller the slices for everyone would be. He did not understand that the more people who come, the more people are able to contribute to make the pie bigger, and the larger everyone's slices would be. It's Economics 101!

Some people would argue that this is just an assumption, but they only need to look at the U.S. history to see the evidence. America is a promised land of opportunities for anyone who has the will and determination. Its history is built by immigrants from all over the world who came to America with nothing other than their willingness to work hard to build a new life for themselves and for their families. I know we did. We have incentives to work, and contribute to the U.S. economy to help it become a richer and stronger country. Of course, not everyone who came here would be successful, but the belief that if they are willing to work hard, there would be plenty of opportunities for them to succeed has always driven people to America.

For example, Jan Koum, co-founder of WhatsApp, came to America when he was sixteen, and his family had to rely on food stamps when they first arrived. Sergey Brin (Russia), co-founder of Google; Do Won Chang (South Korea), co-founder and CEO of Forever 21; Vinod Dham (India), "father of Pentium"; Andy Grove (Hungary), co-founder of Intel Corporation; and Jerry Yang (Taiwan), founder of Yahoo, are just some of many immigrants who came to America with limited or no English and little money, and had to work odd jobs to support themselves before they were successful.

Andrew Ly, founder of Sugar Bowl Bakery, was a refugee from Vietnam. He spent nine months in a refugee camp in Malaysia and was sponsored by the U.S. Catholic Church. His family of eight arrived in America with only a few dollars in their pockets and lived in a two-bed room apartment in San Francisco. In 1984, Ly and his four brothers used their savings to open Sugar Bowl Bakery. Ly's bakery was a big success and became a $400 million corporation. In 1993, Ly Brothers Corporation was founded and Ly was recognized as the "Most Admired CEO" in the San Francisco Bay Area and was awarded the "Immigrant Heritage Award".

I could go on.

In his farewell letter to the nation in 1989, President Ronald Reagan mentioned the story about a big ship, a refugee, and a sailor. In the early eighties, at the height of the boat people crisis, the USS Midway was patrolling the South China Sea, and the crew spotted on the horizon a tiny boat crammed with Vietnamese refugees inside. The Midway sent a large boat to the rescue. When the refugees saw the American crew, one person stood up and yelled to an American sailor: "Hello, American sailor! Hello freedom man!" The American sailor could not help but write this event in a letter to remember the moment. When Reagan heard about the letter, he could not get it out of his mind, either. In his farewell letter, Reagan wrote: "Because that's what it was to be an American in the 1980s. We stood again for freedom. I know we always have, but in the past few years the world again - and in a way, we ourselves - rediscovered it." He went on and called America the "shining city upon a hill", a phrase he borrowed from John Winthrop. He described it as "a tall, proud city built on rocks stronger than oceans, wind-swept, God-blessed, and teeming with people of all kinds living in harmony and peace; a city with free ports that hummed with commerce and creativity. And if there had to be city walls, the walls had doors, and the doors were open to anyone with the will and the heart to get here. That's how I saw it, and see it still."

When I joined the then INS in the early nineties, I often told my colleagues that it was an honor for me to serve in an agency that was responsible not only for the processing and adjudication of immigration applications but also the American dreams of many people. I told them that, back in the eighties when I applied for the N-400, Application for Naturalization, I had to go to the Baltimore District Office very early in the morning to get in a long line, and wait for hours in the cold weather for my interview. I explained how the service had significantly improved because of the agency's investment in moving from a paper-based to a computerized process. I was proud of my contribution to the agency's success and was disappointed when the Trump's administration betrayed the American tradition as a nation of immigrants and did everything they could to undermine the mission of the agency.

The immigration system is undoubtedly broken, and fixing it is easier said than done. Banning entry, closing the border and building a wall did not fix the problem as we had seen. We need a comprehensive solution that is both practical and humane. But throughout my entire career at the immigration agency and five administrations; we went through many planning and preparation for comprehensive immigration reform, and each time Congress failed to come up with a bill which everyone on both sides of the aisle could agree on.

In his book "A Promised Land", Obama wrote: "the economic gulf between us and our southern neighbors drove hundreds of thousands of people to illegally cross the 1,993-mile U.S.-Mexico border each year, searching for work and a better life." But that is not the complete picture. Other factors include government corruption, crime, violence, and climate change are driving migration from countries like El Salvador, Guatemala, and Honduras to the U.S. The U.S needs to work with the governments of those countries to address the root causes of the problems so people don't need to flee their countries. Big U.S. corporations could play a major role; they could export jobs to Central America instead of China, for example. The U.S. government could also stop gun sales that go to the drug cartels and organized crime to reduce crime rate and extortions in those countries.

In 2019, Michelle and I, and a group of friends, took a Panama cruise trip to Central America. We were in awe at the technological marvel of the canal in carrying our 165,000-ton ship up and down through the narrow canal. The Panama Canal generates about $2 billion a year and accounts for more than 30 percent of Panama's annual economic growth, but prosperity is not felt equally by all[21]. More than one quarter of the population lives in poverty. The situation is more or less the same in other countries we visited, such as Honduras, Nicaragua and Columbia. In Honduras, we went to see the banana plantations; most of them were controlled by U.S. based fruit companies such as Dole, United Fruit, and Del Monte. A tour guide

161

told us the Chinese were building a railroad system there in Honduras, and has invested in many infrastructure projects in Latin America. In Ecuador, a senior government official told John Perkins, author of the book "The New Confessions of an Economic Hit Man" that his country would rather borrow money from the Chinese than the Americans, because the Chinese had not overthrown his government or killed his leaders.[22]

While many people in the U.S. feared the illegal immigrants were taking jobs away from them and causing undue burdens on the social services programs, they actually benefited from this silent workforce. Many of the illegal immigrants worked on farms, construction sites, cleaning and landscaping services for subpar pay. And many actually were paying taxes on benefits they could never receive, such as social security and others.

There are between 11 and 13 million undocumented people in the U.S., most people would think they all come from the southern border. The fact is about 40% came here legally on tourist, business or student visas and overstayed. There is no effective way to track this population and the U.S. government still does not know the exact number or the whereabouts of these people. All 19 of the 9/11 terrorists came to this country legally through the front door with some overstayed their visas, and none came from the southern border despite the rhetoric from the right-wing extremists.

In 1996, I drove my mother to Baltimore for her naturalization interview; she had worried that her English was not good enough although she had studied, and prepared hard for the test at home. After the interview, I asked the immigration officer whether she passed the test, and he looked at me and said:

"How could I fail her? She was such a sweet and remarkable lady!"

I was delighted and thanked the officer. I did not tell him I also worked for the agency to avoid any appearance that I was looking for any favor. I was proud of my mother for passing the test to become a U.S. citizen and achieving her American dream.

After our second daughter, Courtney, was born in 1997, my mother had a series of mini stroke. The doctors said they were Transient Ischemic Attacks (TIAs) causing by a condition called atrial fibrillation (AFib). She had to take the blood thinner drug to reduce the risk of blood clots and was recovering well through regular physical therapy. In August 1998, however, she suffered a massive stroke and never regained consciousness. The doctors were not sure what caused the hemorrhage; they suspected she might have fallen during the day when no one was at home.

She was with us for exactly 16 years since our family was reunited, and I would trade anything just to have her back again, even just for a day.

THE LITTLE PRINCE

One weekend, after our daughter Nikki moved out a few years ago, I went to her room to clear out the clutter of her books and school papers that had accumulated all the way back from elementary through high school. As I was going through her bookshelf, I found a homework folder about a reading assignment that we had worked on together when she was still in elementary school. It included our write-ups and her teacher's comments about the book "The Little Prince" by Antoine de St. Exupéry. It was a project that her teacher had assigned to students and parents to work on together by picking a book to read and writing our thoughts about it separately. I chose "The Little Prince" since I remembered reading it as a child and thought it would be an interesting book for her to read. Little did I know at the time that my understanding and perspective of the book when I read it again as an adult would be so different from when I was a kid, and because of this, I appreciated it so much more.

"The Little Prince" is a children's book written by

Antoine de Saint-Exupéry. It was not a coincidence that one of the elementary schools I attended in Saigon in the sixties was also named after him. Saint-Exupéry was a renowned writer and a successful commercial pilot before World War II. In 1935, during an attempt to break the speed record in a Paris-to-Saigon air race, Saint-Exupéry and his navigator crashed in the Libyan desert. They survived the crash but suffered severe dehydration and hallucinations in the intense desert heat. It was, perhaps, during this near-death experience that Saint-Exupéry came up with the idea about the book "The Little Prince", as a reflection of his life while being stranded in the desert. However, he did not write the book until 1943, during his two-year self-imposed exile from Nazi-occupied France.

Nonetheless, it was a wonderful and beautifully written book, not only for children, but for adults as well. Each character that the little prince encountered on the planets he visited represented a type of personality we could find in our everyday life: the astronomer, the king, the vain man, the drunkard, the businessman, the lamplighter, the geographer, the snake, the fox, and even the flower that was the love of his life. Just like the little prince who left his beautiful rose to go on his journey to visit other planets, the author left his wife to go on his many trips, since his job as a pilot took him to different countries around the world, where he would meet other women, but in the end, he would always come back to her.

The book had a sad ending in which the little prince died because he let the snake bite him; he said he had traveled too far away from his planet and it would be difficult for him to go back to his rose because his body would be too heavy to fly. About a year after the author wrote "The Little Prince," during a reconnaissance mission flight over occupied France, his airplane disappeared and was never found.

This book has so many messages and wisdom requiring deeper interpretations at different levels that we all could learn from. As I read the book again many decades later, I could not put it down, and I had to read it again a couple more times to make sure that I did not miss any hidden messages. Such a small and powerful book that both children and adults could read and enjoy, yet with different interpretations. It was certainly enjoyable for me.

The following excerpts do not include all the messages in this little book, but they are certainly the ones that stood out the most to me:

"Grown-ups are unnecessarily complicated." As a child, the narrator was not too impressed with the grown-ups; even after he grew up and became a pilot and traveled the world, he still talked about grown-ups in the third person plural. "They" were always too serious, according to the narrator. When I read "The Little Prince" again as an adult, it changed the way I interacted with my daughters; I tried to see things through their lenses to understand their needs. As parents, we often get caught up in our own world and expect our children to behave the way we see things; "The Little Prince" certainly changed my perspective, and I believe it has made me a better father.

"People are judged by the way they dress." When

the narrator learned about the tiny planet where the little prince came from, he believed it was called "Asteroid B-612". A Turkish Astronomer who spotted in 1909 made a formal announcement of his discovery at the International Astronomical Congress. No one believed him, however, because of the way he was dressed. When he was ordered by the Turkish dictator to wear European clothes, only then did everyone believe him, although he had given the same announcement. We are often told not to judge a book by its cover, but in real life, people always do that. I had a colleague who was a Mexican American, and he always wore a suit and tie to go to work, even on Fridays, which were casual days. I asked him why he always dressed up and he said:

"I am from Mexico and I used to live in Texas, where people often mistook me for an illegal immigrant. It seemed when I dressed professionally, I would not get harassed as often."

"Grown-ups like numbers" - When meeting a new friend, the grown-ups in The Little Prince were not concerned about what the friend was like or what his interests were; they only wanted to know things like how much money his father made, or when talking about a house, grown-ups ignored the house's beautiful red brick with beautiful flowers, but once they heard the house was worth a hundred thousand francs, they all exclaimed "What a beautiful house!" We live in a materialistic world; I have seen too many people who are excessively obsessed with material possessions, such as a nice car, a big house, and a high-paying job. In the end, once you close your eyes, they will all become meaningless.

"It is much harder to judge yourself than to judge

others." On his first planet, the little prince met a king who reigned over a tiny planet, but who was also a wise man. The king said judging oneself is "the hardest thing of all. It is much harder to judge yourself than to judge others. If you succeed in judging yourself, it's because you are truly a wise man." One important verse in the Bible said that you should judge yourself first before judging others, but I have not met too many people who have been actually able to do that, whether intentionally or unintentionally. My mother used to say that you should twist your tongue seven times before you speak, or if you have nothing nice to say, then say nothing at all. One of her favorite old sayings was: "Words do not cost you money, so you should choose your words to please one another."

"Vain men are pitiful because they are insecure and so they need to be praised" - On the second planet, the little prince saw a very vain man. He constantly needed to be praised for everything about himself: he wanted to be called the handsomest, best dressed, richest, and most intelligent, even though he was the only one on his entire planet. He spent of all his time praising and admiring himself. When a person lives for the admiration of others, he never lives for himself, and therefore he does not care for or concern about others. There are many people like this vain man who live on our planet, but one in particular stands out and we all know who this man is. He was the one who claimed to be "the richest man in America," "the greatest deal maker," "the greatest president since Abraham Lincoln"; everything about him had to be the best - smartest, best looking, biggest buildings, biggest crowd. I wonder: if the little prince had met him, what would he think of this "great" man?

"Never take yourself too seriously." A businessman who lived on the fourth planet was a serious man. His job was to count and recount all the stars all day and all year round so that he could own them. He told the little prince that he did not have time to exercise or to take strolls, although he had rheumatism. The businessman took his job so seriously that he did not even have time to enjoy all the stars he owned. Many people are married to their jobs; they don't have time to spend with their loved ones or to enjoy life. Harold Kushner once said, "No one ever said on their deathbed - I wish I'd spent more time at the office."

"Don't forget to enjoy life." Just stop whatever you are doing and enjoy the moment. On the fifth planet, the lamplighter who lived there was perhaps the only one among the others whom the little prince might have become friends with, since he was doing something that benefited someone other than himself. His planet was so tiny and turned so quickly that it revolved once per minute. Since the day was only one minute long, he had to light the lamp and turn it off every minute. He had no time to rest. A day went by in a minute, a month in thirty minutes, and a lifetime in a few days.

"Get out and explore the world." The little prince met a geographer on the sixth planet who never went out to explore his own world. He relied on the explorers to tell him about the cities, rivers, mountains, seas, oceans, and deserts, but he did not trust them to tell the truth. Too busy working behind his desk, he lived a boring life.

"And now here is my secret, a very simple secret: It is only with the heart that one can see rightly; what is essential is invisible to the eye." Although the little prince loved and cared deeply about his rose, he was too naïve and did not look beyond the surface to see the affection she had for him since the rose hid her true feelings and pretended that her tiny thorns could protect her when the little prince said he wanted to go to other planets to explore. So away he went, thinking the rose was too proud and did not love him or have the same feelings for him.

"The most beautiful things in the world cannot be seen or touched, they are felt with the heart." My mother never finished high school, but she was full of wisdom, and I learned a lot from her. She always said character trumps physical beauty; it does not matter how beautiful a person looks, but if he or she has no character, then that person is just a walking statue. It is the inner beauty that cannot be seen or touched that is more important. Another favorite quote from my mother was: "It is better to have quality wood than shiny paint."

"People where you live," the little prince said, "grow five thousand roses in one garden... Yet they don't find what they're looking for... And yet what they're looking for could be found in a single rose." Many people spend their entire lives looking for something, not realizing that what they had been looking for was right in front of them the entire time.

"If you love a flower that lives in a star, it is sweet to look at the sky at night. All the stars are abloom with flowers." The message is: love is blind. If you love someone, then anywhere that person lives would be beautiful. The opposite is also true. There is an old Vietnamese saying that goes something like; when you love someone, you love even the road that the person walks on, and when you hate someone, you hate his or her entire bloodline.

"One day, I watched the sun setting forty-four times... You know... when one is so terribly sad, one loves sunsets." Nguyen Du, a well-known Vietnamese poet and author of the epic poem "The Tale of Kiều," wrote: "When you are sad, the surrounding environment would never be cheerful." People are more attuned to something melancholy when they are sad.

"It is the time you have wasted for your rose that makes your rose so important." Hrithik Roshan once said, "Patience is the mother of all virtues," and Jean-Jacques Rousseau also wrote, "Patience is bitter, but its fruit is sweet." It is the time and effort that you spend to do or achieve something that makes it priceless; you value it more than something you would receive for free. People spend money more freely when they win a lottery or when they do not have to work for it. I have read many stories about people who had won the lottery, and most of them ended up poor again because they had spent all their money recklessly to enjoy the moment and did not invest or plan for the future.

"It's a little lonely in the desert," the Little Prince said. The fox said, "It is lonely when you're among people, too". Loneliness is a state of mind; sometimes you can feel just as lonely in a room full of people as you do when you are alone by yourself. Choose your friends, and spend time with those who make you feel comfortable, but more importantly, be yourself - be your own friend so you don't feel lonely even if you are alone.

And here is the letter I wrote to my daughter Nikki as part of her homework.

Dear Nicole,

I first read The Little Prince when I was about your age; would you believe it was more than 35 years ago? The book I read, however, was in French and it was called Le Petit Prince. I only had a vague memory about the book, but I remembered I had enjoyed reading it.

Although it was supposedly written for children but as an adult reading it again after so many years, I found it very interesting and that I probably did not understand it the way I do now. There are so many messages in the book that even for me now to learn and appreciate when I re-read it. The English version is simple in the choice of words and easy to understand. I hope you will also enjoy it as much as I did.

Love,
Dad

And here is the letter from her teacher.

Dear Nicole,

I enjoyed reading the letters that you and your father wrote on "The Little Prince". Like your father, I read this book as a young person in both English and French. It was interesting to read your father's comment that the translated version (English) lost some elements of originality and effectiveness. As a student in high school, I realized that even though the book appears as if it is written for children (simplistic writing and illustrations), it is actually for both children and adults. This is one of the points your father mentioned in his first letter to you. It is one of those books that people can re-read throughout their lifetime and understand deeper levels of meanings (sort of like peeling away layers of onion).

It was wonderful for me to read your journal, for it represented a young person's and a grown-up's interpretations. I think you and Dad had wonderful insights, and you inspired me to take my copy of "The Little Prince" off my bookshelf and re-read it this weekend. Like your father, it's been a couple of decades (I can't believe it!) since I last read this. I loved re-reading it, and I understood the messages in the book in a different way, since my perception lens has changed. I hope you will pick this book up again throughout your lifetime and compare your thoughts to those in your journal as an 8 years old girl. Keep your journal!

Ms. T.

SEPTEMBER 11

It was a beautiful September morning with a clear blue sky. Schools in Virginia had been reopened for over a week and the football season had also just begun. The Washington Redskins just lost their season opener to the San Diego Chargers on Sunday, September 9th, 2001. Life was as normal as it could be in the nation's capital, except for the somber mood that persisted every time the home team lost a game. The Washington football team no longer resembled its glory days of the eighties when it had won two Super Bowls. The last time they won the championship was in January 1991.

After dropping our daughters Courtney at day care and Nikki at Oakton Elementary school, I drove to work in D.C. with my wife, Michelle, as usual. Traffic on Route 50 East that day was heavier than normal due to people going back to school and work, but nothing was out of the ordinary. We passed by the iconic Iwo Jima War Memorial and merged onto the exit ramp to the

Theodore Roosevelt bridge. As we crossed the bridge, I took the exit to Constitution Avenue and headed toward the U.S. Capitol. When we approached the Ellipse, the White House appeared on the left behind the rows of trees from afar across a long green lawn. President George W. Bush, the new occupant at the White House since January, was away in Florida. He was scheduled to visit an elementary school in Saratoga. From Constitution Avenue, we turned left and headed toward Chinatown. As it happened, Michelle and I worked at the two buildings across from each other near the Renaissance Hotel in Chinatown at the time. It was approximately 8:00 am when we pulled into the underground garage of the building.

After settling down at my desk, I went down to the basement coffee shop of the Renaissance Hotel with Hugh J., a colleague, to get coffee. Hugh was a Vietnam vet; he spent one year in Quang Ngai from September 1968 to August 1969 and served in a field artillery unit to provide fire support for military operations and the defense of the Quang Ngai airfield and army base about four kilometers west of Quang Ngai. Although he spent one year in Vietnam, Hugh stayed inside the base most of the time he was there. When he was on R&R, he went to Australia where he met his future wife. The only time he ever saw any Vietnamese people, ironically, was when the Viet-Cong attacked the firebase and some of them were captured as prisoners of war. These Viet-Cong soldiers were actually a specially trained North Vietnamese Army (NVA) assault forces called "sapper" by U.S. forces. They were the elite NVA units and most feared by Americans. They normally operated in three- and six-man teams.

With their bodies covered with charcoal dust and grease that made them almost invisible in the dark; they silently slipped through the barbed wired around the perimeter of the firebase under the umbrella of NVA mortar fire and raced through the base, tossing grenades from their canvas satchel bags. They rarely carry firearms; their only weapons were the bags loaded with grenades and explosives that they carried across their bodies.

While waiting to get our coffees that day, Hugh and I followed the news on a TV screen nearby. At around 8:45 am, CNN stopped the regular program to announce breaking news that an American Airlines plane had crashed into one of the World Trade Center (WTC) twin buildings in New York City. Everyone's eyes were fixed on the replayed image of American Flight 11 crashing into the North Tower and exploding into a giant ball of fire. At the time, we all thought that it was a terrible accident - then when we saw a second plane, United Airlines Flight 175, hit the South Tower, we all watched in horror. Hugh immediately told me, "This is definitely not an accident! We are under attack."

A crowd had gathered around the TV screen to follow the news in disbelief. While everyone was watching, CNN reported a third plane, American Airlines Flight 77, had crashed into the West side of the Pentagon in Arlington, Virginia. I thought, "My God, it's getting closer to home!" The TV screen then switched back to New York City and showed images of people jumping out of the twin towers' windows and falling to their deaths because they could not stand the intense heat. One after another, people dropped like flies. It was so horrific. The WTC twin towers prior to the terrorist attacks were considered being the tallest buildings in the world, measuring at 1,638 feet and 1,362 feet tall. Then the towers collapsed; first the North Tower, then the South Tower, crumbling down like broken pancakes. As a combat soldier in Vietnam, Hugh said that he had experienced and seen death close up and even heard some of his fellow soldiers scream from being burned alive during NVA/Vietcong attacks, but watching innocent people trapped on top floors jumping to their deaths rather than waiting to die in the inferno on a TV screen was surreal and shocking.

We went back up to the office to see if there were any announcements from our management. Standing on the eighth floor of the Tech World building, I could see a billow of black smoke from the direction of the Pentagon in contrast to the blue sky. The image triggered my memory and feeling of another attack on April 28, 1975 when we stood on the third floor of the Duy Tan apartment complex in Saigon and looked at the columns of smoke from Tan Son Nhut Air Base, an image that I thought I would never see again, let alone in the capital of the U.S.

At around 11:00 am, everyone was told to gather on the eighth floor to hear the updates from the agency leadership. We were told to stay put to wait for further instructions. There were rumors about a fourth plane on its way to Washington, D.C. with the White House or the U.S. Capitol as the target. We heard that two F-15s were deployed to shoot down the airplane if it entered the D.C. air space. We also heard that a car bomb was discovered near the Department of State building at Foggy Bottom, but it was later confirmed to be not correct. The Office of

Personnel Management (OPM) decided that all U.S. government buildings in the D.C. area could be targets for terrorist attacks, and that the cost of human lives would be higher if everyone stayed in their collective locations, so it decided to send everyone home. The order was for everyone to leave in an orderly fashion, but as soon as the instructions were sent out, everyone left almost at the same time, creating a deadlock on the streets of the nation's capital.

I tried to call Michelle but could not get through - all phone lines, including cellular signals, were jammed up. Since her building was just across the street, I walked over to get her, and we tried to get out of D.C. However, it took us almost two hours just to get out of the city. The traffic was congested everywhere, but eventually we were able to get out and get home after picking up our daughters.

Once at home, we turned on the TV to get the latest status. Preliminary reports described a group of terrorists who hijacked large aircraft with full loads of fuel at the East coast airports and were bound for the West coast. Their intention was to turn those aircraft into giant flying bombs to inflict maximum damage and destruction. The Federal Aviation Administration (FAA) grounded all flights across the U.S. airspace for the first time in U.S. aviation history. It was reported that a fourth plane, United Airlines Flight 93, had crashed into an empty field near Shanksville, Pennsylvania. The detailed report revealed that the passengers on the United Airlines plane attacked the hijackers in an attempt to retake control of the plane. The plane eventually crashed into a field in western Pennsylvania about eighty miles from Pittsburgh.

On that morning, President Bush was reading to a group of second graders in a classroom in Saratoga, Florida. He was quickly escorted to Airforce One and flew to Offutt Airforce Base, the headquarters of the U.S. Strategic Command (USSTRATCOM) in Nebraska. At Offutt, Bush declared: "We are at war."

Investigations by the U.S. indicated that the Islamic militant group al-Qaeda was responsible for the attacks. The group was famous for their coordinated attacks on hitting multiple targets at the same time. Their leader, Osama bin Laden, had previously made many anti-American threats. In 1998, bin Laden had declared a holy war against the United States. At the time of the 9/11 attacks, bin Laden was in Afghanistan and was protected by the country's ruling militia Taliban. After the U.S. and allied military forces attacked and invaded Afghanistan, bin Laden went into hiding in Pakistan. In his 2002 Letter to America, bin Laden listed the reasons for his attacks to include the continued U.S. support for Israel in its suppression of the Muslims in Lebanon, and the presence of U.S. troops in Saudi Arabia, On May 2, 2011 bin Laden was killed by the U.S. Navy SEALs during a raid on his compound in Pakistan after nearly a ten-year manhunt.

Hugh later told me that his neighbors, a husband and wife, were on the plane that crashed into the Pentagon. Another neighbor, who drove them to Dulles airport, said they were on their way to L.A. and then to Hawaii. They were taking her father's ashes to be scattered at Pearl Harbor. Her father was a sailor during World War II and survived the attack on December 7th, 1941. This neighbor was devastated since not only she lost two friends but also because she could not fulfill her father's last wish; his ashes ended up in the rubble at the Pentagon instead of at Pearl Harbor. One day, she just packed up and moved because she could not bear the pain everyday looking at the house where her couple friends used to live.

A Vietnamese American, Khang Nguyen, working at the Pentagon as a civilian system engineer for the U.S. Navy also perished that day. His son was only four when he lost his father. The son was part of a new generation that has grown up over the last two decades, with vague memories of their parents who died on September 11.

The September 11 attacks were not the first time terrorists had targeted the World Trade Center. On February 26, 1993, a group of terrorists detonated a truck bomb below the North Tower, intending to crash that tower into the South Tower to bring both towers down and kill thousands of people. The bomb exploded in the underground garage and created a 100-ft wide hole through four sublevels of concrete.
[23] It killed six people and injured over one thousand. However, the North Tower did not collapse as planned by the terrorists. The investigation revealed that had the truck been parked closer to the WTC's poured concrete foundations, their plan might have succeeded. The mastermind behind the first WTC bombing was a Pakistani man named Ramzi Yousef, who came to the U.S. with a fake Iraqi passport. After the bombing, Yousef escaped to Pakistan.

In January 1995, Yousef and Khalid Sheikh Mohammed traveled to the Philippines and planned a large scale, three-phase terrorist attack which they called

"Operation Bojinka." During the first phase, they planned to assassinate Pope John Paul II during his visit to the Philippines on January 15, 1995. In the next phase, they would place bombs on 11 U.S.-bound planes and have them explode simultaneously over the Pacific Ocean and the South China Sea. If the plan had been executed, thousands of people would have been killed. The last phase involved a terrorist flying a small rented airplane filled with explosives and crashing it into the Central Intelligence Agency headquarters in Langley, Virginia. The terrorists had probably studied the Japanese kamikaze suicidal attacks in World War II in which the pilots would crash their airplanes loaded with explosives into U.S. battleships. There were alternate plans in which the terrorists planned to hijack commercial airplanes instead of small aircraft and crash them into multiple targets in the U.S., such as the World Trade Center, the Pentagon, the U.S. Capitol, the White House, the Sears Tower, and the U.S. Bank Tower.

By pure luck, Yousef and his accomplices had to abandon the Bojinka plot was because of a chemical fire that one terrorist accidentally started in an apartment kitchen sink. Although the fire went out on its own, the Philippines police decided to investigate the situation after residents reported suspicious activities. Yousef and Abdul Hakim Murad, the terrorist who started the fire, had fled the scene, but they had left behind evidence of bomb making material, a manual written in Arabic on how to make liquid bombs, detailed plans of Operation Bojinka including the Pope's schedule, street maps of Manila with routes of the papal motorcade, and Yousef's laptop containing flight schedules and other items in the hard drive. The text in one file on the hard drive stated: "All people who support the U.S. government are our targets in our future plans and that is because all those people are responsible for their government's actions and they support the U.S. foreign policy and are satisfied with it. We will hit all U.S. nuclear targets. If the U.S. government keeps supporting Israel, then we will continue to carry out operations inside and outside the United States..."

Murad was captured by the Philippines police and confessed after he was told that he would be sent to Israel to be interrogated by the Mossad, the national intelligence agency of Israel, if he did not cooperate. Yousef again escaped to Pakistan but was captured by the Pakistani Inter-Services Intelligence (ISI) and U.S. Diplomatic Security Service after a 23-day manhunt and was extradited to the U.S. The Philippines consequently forwarded all information about the Bojinka plot to the FBI in April 1995. Yousef was convicted in a U.S. Court and received two life sentences plus 240 years for his part in the 1993 World Trade Center bombing and Bojinka plot. The plot to use commercial airplanes to crash into targets was eventually executed during the September 11 attacks, although only the World Trade Center and the Pentagon were hit.

In 2006, we went to Ground Zero in New York City to see the location where it happened. At the time, all we saw was a giant hole in the ground and fences put up all around the site, but the eerie feeling was unmistakable. This was where nearly 3,000 lives were lost in the deadliest attack on U.S. soil since Pearl Harbor.

While we were in New York City, we walked around the section of lower Broadway and the Financial District, and we noticed a marker on one sidewalk embedded with South Vietnam President Ngo Dinh Diem's name to commemorate his visit to the United States in 1957. I was surprised and curious to see his name on a sidewalk in New York City, so I did a little research and learned that President Dwight Eisenhower invited Diem to the U.S. where he received a glowing welcome and was praised as "The Winston Churchill of Southeast Asia." President Eisenhower personally greeted him at the airport. In Washington, D.C., Diem addressed the U.S. Congress and was heartily received by both sides of the aisles. In New York City, he was given a ticker tape parade through Manhattan, which 250,000 people attended. It was a stark contrast to his tragic end when he was overthrown and murdered by his own generals.

Ground Zero, WTC September 11, 2001 Attack
(Author's Collection)

WTC February 26, 1993 Attack.
(Author's Collection)

President Ngo Dinh Diem's ticker-tape parade marker in NYC.
(Author's Collection)

President Eisenhower greets Diem at the airport. *(nsarchive2.gw.edu–Timetoast)*

President Diem in New York City. *(Photo by Carl T. Gossett Jr/New York Times Co./Getty Images)*

WASHINGTON, D.C.

If Paris is known as the city of love, then
Washington, D.C. is known as the city of power, and
politics, where decisions can shape and unshape world
events. It is also a city full of conspiracy theories and spy
activities. Here you won't find lovers walking arm in arm
along the Tidal Basin or the Potomac River. You also
won't find famous authors or poets visiting for inspiration
to write romantic stories or lovely poems like you would
at the Luxembourg Gardens in Paris. The city breathes
politics. In the street, you're more likely to hear a young
couple out on their first date asking each other, "Are you
a Republican or a Democrat?" rather than "Do you like
rock or country music?"

However, that does not mean Washington, D.C.
does not have its own beauty and charm as a powerful
city. After all, it was designed and built by Pierre
L'Enfant, a French architect, based on models of other
European cities such as Paris and Amsterdam. As the

capital city of the United States, it is home to all three branches of the federal government, including the White House, the Supreme Court, and the Capitol Building. It is also home to many other famous landmarks, such as the Washington Monument, Lincoln Monument, and the National Cathedral, among others.

During the past few decades, Washington, D.C. has transformed a lot with cool new neighborhoods, award-winning restaurants to attract visitors, and people from Maryland and Virginia who come to work and live here. One of the biggest changes was the "clean-up program" that got rid of areas such as "Hooker Alley," which I remember back in the seventies and eighties, had many Go-Go Bars, X-Rated movie theaters and the 14 Street N.W. corridor that was full of sex workers, which was just a couple blocks away from the White House. These former areas did not project the "nice" image of the capital of the United States to leaders, and dignitaries from other countries who came here for a visit or meeting at the White House.

When I was in college during the late seventies, I worked part time at a Japanese restaurant in Georgetown, a French quarter in Northwest D.C. During the weekend nights when I got off from work, I usually hung out with a few friends at places like Café de Paris, Au Pied de Cochon, and Crazy Horse, and, I admit, that sometimes we went to Good Guys, a popular Go-Go place on Wisconsin Avenue. At the time, there were only two Vietnamese restaurants located right next to each other on M Street. We usually went there for a taste of the old Saigon.

Georgetown was also a frequent place for some

famous people from Hollywood to enjoy a night out. I
saw Marlon Brando, Elizabeth Taylor, Jane Fonda, and
her late husband Tom Hayden in our Japanese restaurant
quite a few times. The scene in which Father Karras falls
down the high staircase in "The Exorcist" was shot near
Georgetown University on M Street and Prospect. That
area is always dark and creepy, and it still gives me a
spooky feeling every time I walk by it.

Like any other big cities in the U.S., Washington,
D.C. also has a Chinatown, but it is slowly disappearing,
and soon the only thing left standing is the giant
Chinatown Friendship Archway. The giant archway was
constructed in 1986 as a joint project between the two
cities, Washington D.C. and Beijing, after Mayor Marion
Barry visited the China's capital. The idea behind the
project was to create a visible attraction to serve as a
magnet for visitors. Today, there are still a few Chinese
restaurants and shops on H Street, but otherwise the
entire area has been transformed around the Capital One
Arena with new restaurants and pubs. We used to go to
Chinatown to eat after late night partying at the
Vietnamese night clubs. It was the only place that stayed
open late for the hungry souls looking for something to
eat.

After graduating from college in 1982, I worked for
the private sectors for a while, then I joined the federal
service in the early nineties. Michelle also found a job
with the federal government, and so for nearly thirty years
we commuted to Washington, D.C. together to work
every day. I had come to love the extraordinary city with
its multicultural, and diverse personalities, but I also hated
its traffic. It would take me thirty minutes to drive from

Virginia to D.C., but once I entered the city, I could easily spend one hour stuck in a gridlock.

At lunch time, I used to walk around the U.S. Capitol Building with my colleague Joe Holliday. I have never been inside the Capitol; the closest I have ever been to it, was walking up to the stairs from the West side so that I could see the Reflecting Pool, the Washington Monument, and the Lincoln Monument from miles away. The U.S. Capitol is among the most architecturally impressive buildings in the world, and symbolically important for what it stands for: democracy and freedom. On top of the dome of the Capitol is the Statue of Freedom; it is a bronze statue designed by Thomas Crawford in 1863. People from around the world are familiar with the Statue of Liberty on Ellis Island in New York Harbor, but not too many know about the Statue of Freedom, including myself, until Joe pointed it out to me. Joe explained it may look small from the ground level, but it is almost 20 feet tall and weighs 15,000 pounds.

I also liked to go to one of the senate buildings to eat lunch at the cafeteria there with my colleagues, and once in a while we would spot some U.S. senators there. When I had more time, I liked to walk along the National Mall, which is a rectangular park about two miles long between Constitution and Independence Avenue. On both sides of the Mall are the Smithsonian museums, comprising seventeen museums and galleries. I have not been to all of them, but some of my favorite museums are: The National Air and Space Museum, National Museum of American History, American Art Museum and Renwick Gallery, National Portrait Gallery, and National Museum of Natural History where you can see the biggest diamond in the world. The unique thing about the Smithsonian museums is that they are free; you don't need to buy a ticket, unlike any other museum in the world. Even at the Louvre in Paris, only the first Sunday of the month is free. When we visited Paris in 2012, we went to the Louvre on a Sunday and it was free, but all the spectacular water fountains were turned off to save money.

Beside the Smithsonian museums, there are other museums that are not a part of the Smithsonian Institute, and require buying admission tickets, such as the International Spy Museum, the National Geographic Museum, the National Building Museum, and the Newseum, but they are still worthwhile to see. The Newseum, however, was closed in 2019, and will be relocated to an undetermined location.

Near the Lincoln Memorial is the Vietnam Veterans Memorial where over 58,000 names of U.S. soldiers who died during the Vietnam War are engraved on a long black granite wall. I come here once in a while to pay tribute to the men and women who sacrificed their lives to protect the freedom and democracy of our native country in the fight against communism.

The World War II Memorial and the Korean War Veterans Memorial are also located here. Near the Tidal Basin is the Martin Luther King Jr. Memorial, it was dedicated in 2011 after over two decades of planning, fundraising, and construction. Dr. King was the prominent leader of the Civil Rights Movement, in which he advocated non-violent resistance inspired by Mahatma Gandhi. His "I Have a Dream" speech was ranked the top American speech of the twentieth century in a 1999 poll of scholars of public address.

The most interesting place in Washington, D.C. for me, is the Library of Congress. It is considered the biggest library in the world, comprising three buildings on Capitol Hill. It has over three million books of different types in over 450 different languages, and millions of other documents stored in microfilms, world maps, and music sheets, among others. The purpose of the library is to serve members of the U.S. Congress, but it is also open to the public. However, only congressional staff and government employees can check out books. When I was still working as a federal employee, I had a Library of Congress card, and I used to go there to do research to write my grandfather's Wikipedia page. During my research, I came across the book "Le Dragon d'Annam" written by Bao Dai, the last Emperor of Vietnam. I saw the same book listed on Amazon for over $300.

Another well know landmark in D.C. is the Watergate. If it were not for the Watergate scandal, the Watergate would be just an ordinary building complex comprising six buildings that are used for office space, a hotel, cooperative apartments, and also the headquarters for the Democratic National Committee (DNC). This is where the break-in happened that led to the resignation of President Richard Nixon because of his administration's continuous attempts to cover up its involvement in the break-in and, subsequently, the impeachment process against him. Nixon resigned before he was ever actually impeached by the House. The Watergate is near the Potomac River, next to the John F. Kennedy Center for the Performing Arts, which is where theater, dance, ballet, orchestral, jazz, popular, and folk music are performed.

When Michelle's family resettled in the

Washington, D.C. area in 1975, her whole family worked in the kitchen at the Watergate Hotel. Michelle recounted she had to wake up very early in the morning to go to work with her family. She fell asleep in the family car during the short drive from Virginia to D.C. because she was not used to wake up at the early hours. She often came home after work crying because she felt a lady working there always yelled at her. Eventually, she quit to go to college, hoping to have a better future. Her family, however, continued to work at the hotel. During that time, her father studied the pastry chef while he was making all kinds of different mouthwatering French pastries in the hotel's kitchen. Ever a proud entrepreneur and successful businessman in Saigon himself, he eventually created and recorded his own recipes for all the famous French pastries based on what he learned. Then one day, he wrote a long letter saying thank you and goodbye to the hotel management staff and walked out with his family. He opened his own bakery shop in Springfield, Virginia and named it "Le Blédo". I thought it was clever the way he played with words; "Le Blé" is the French word for wheat and "do" is for "dough". "Le Blédo" simply means "wheat dough". For nearly two decades, the bakery provided the sole source of income to put food on the table and support for the whole family.

In 1990, shortly after we got married, I got laid off and out of a job. It was the first time since I got out of college that I was jobless. After several months and only a few interviews with no job offers, I felt restless. During this time, Michelle's father wanted to sell his bakery to retire. The bakery was a family business, but he felt it was time to sell. I thought about taking over the bakery to do something different. Michelle and I had some savings; we could put down and get a bank loan to buy his bakery. Just when I was contemplating with the idea, I received a job offer as a system programmer with the D.C. Superior Court. After discussing with Michelle, I felt I needed a stable income as we just started a family. Becoming a bakery owner and pastry chef sounded pretty cool, but I had no experience. Not only I had to learn to bake cake, I also need to learn how to run the bakery. I would need to hire people, which means I would need capitals which I did not have. In short, I took the job offer and abandoned the dream of becoming a pastry chef.

During the fall, Washington, D.C. is vibrant with beautiful colors from the foliage at Rock Creek Park. I don't need to drive two hours to see the fall foliage on the Skyline drive in Virginia. Here in D.C., Rock Creek Park offers an amazing spot for fall colors, and is picture-perfect for fall hiking in D.C. George Washington Memorial Parkway is also beautiful during the fall; driving on the parkway, I feel like I am driving in the Shenandoah Valley surrounded with stunning colors of red, yellow, and orange leaves along the Potomac River. I often see people jogging, biking, and canoeing on one side of the parkway. On the Virginia side, there is an exit to Langley, the site of the Central Intelligence Agency (CIA) headquarters. I had been there a few times to attend meetings related to our immigration system. When I passed by the traffic stop at the entrance to the CIA, I could not help to think about an incident in 1993, when a Pakistani man named Mir Qazi shot and killed two and wounded three CIA employees while they were stopped at the traffic light. Qazi escaped, and it took four years for the U.S. government to find and capture him in Pakistan through the combined efforts between the FBI and the CIA. He was extradited to the U.S. to stand trial for the murder charges, and received the death penalty. He was executed by lethal injection in 2002.

Speaking of the FBI and CIA, many people still remember the two espionage cases that shook America: Aldrich Ames at the CIA, and Robert Hanssen at the FBI. Ames and Hanssen sold thousands of classified materials to the Russians. These were the worst betrayal cases that caused the most damage in U.S. history of intelligence and counter-intelligence. Ames was a thirty-one-year-old veteran CIA officer who had been spying for the KGB since 1985. He was arrested in 1994 and sentenced to life without parole. Robert Hanssen was a former FBI double agent who spied for the Russians from 1979 to 2001. He was arrested in 2001 and sentenced to fifteen life-terms without the possibility of parole. The location where Hanssen was arrested when he dropped off his packages for the Soviets was Foxstone Park in Vienna. It was the park I passed by every weekend while driving my daughter Courtney to her soccer practices when she was a little girl.

The Washington D.C. area offers four distinct seasons and the winter here can be very cold with the average temperature in the 30s. January is usually the coldest month, and it is also when D.C. gets most of its snow during this time. Although snowstorms of over five inches a day don't happen often, every five to ten years or so, the D.C. area gets a major snowstorm that dumps ten inches or more.

During the Christmas holiday in 1993, we went to

my sister Mai's place in Laurel, Maryland, for a family gathering. Our daughter Nikki was just born about a month before. While we were there, the national weather service issued a snow and ice storm warning for the entire Washington D.C. metropolitan area that evening. Not wanting to get stuck in Maryland, I decided to leave quickly, with the hope of beating the storm before it got worse.

We made it to the Cabin John bridge; also known as the American Legion Memorial Bridge, which is the border between Maryland and Virginia when I blew a rear tire. The freezing temperature had caused the snow to turn into ice as soon as it fell on the road, making it an extremely treacherous condition. The situation became more dangerous when we were on the bridge, since the freezing surface caused cars to lose friction quickly. I had to maintain a constant speed by keeping the gas pedal steady to avoid the car from skidding out of control. Unfortunately, everything had turned into a sheet of ice, and our car would not move forward regardless of how much or how little I pressed on the gas. As the wheels were spinning helplessly, one of the tires gave out. Leaving my wife and Nikki inside the car, I got out after turning the emergency lights on to replace the tire. I hoped other cars would not slam into ours since we were right in the middle of the bridge.

We did not get very far as the spare tire also went flat. I got out of the car and hopelessly waved at other passing vehicles for help, but no one would stop. They were all afraid that if they stopped, their cars would lose momentum, and they could not get them moving again. I realized we were on our own.

As the minutes and hours passed, the snow fell heavier and the temperature colder. I stopped waving and went back inside the car to keep warm. I had worried that the car might soon run out of gas, and I needed to make a quick decision of whether I should try to walk to the next exit to get help. I quickly dismissed the idea since the next exit would be the Georgetown Pike, a few miles away, and I would not be able to find any help there. It would be too dangerous to walk in the frigid temperature, and to leave Michelle and our infant child alone in the car. Meanwhile, Michelle snugged the blanked around Nikki to keep her warm, occasionally repeating a prayer. By that time, the bridge which carries Interstate 495 across the Potomac River was completely empty and the snow was still falling. I found myself helpless, not knowing what to do, so we just sat in the car with the engine running. I do not know how long we stayed in the car when suddenly I saw the headlights of a car coming from afar in the rearview mirror. I jumped out of our vehicle and desperately waved at the incoming car. As it got closer, I saw it was a Maryland state cruiser. I told Michelle, "Thank God, we are safe now! It's a Maryland state police car!"

After realizing our dire situation, the trooper let us stay in his car while he tried to radio for help. Since he was a Maryland state trooper, he explained, it would be out of jurisdiction for him to take us to Virginia. I do not remember how long we were sitting in his car while he was trying repeatedly to radio for help, to no avail. As Nikki became restless and cried, I suggested the trooper take us to the next exit so we could check in to a hotel. Reluctantly but graciously, he agreed. "It's Christmas, I guess it's ok to break the rule", he said.

The trooper took us to the Tysons Corner exit in Virginia and we checked into a Marriott hotel for the night. We were so grateful to the state trooper as we knew he went out of his way to help us. I thought to myself it must be my guardian angel who sent the trooper to help us, and it would certainly be an anecdote to tell our family at every Christmas gathering about an unforgettable Christmas night, albeit one Nikki was too young at the time to have any memory of.

The best time in D.C. is unarguably during the spring when thousands of cherry blossoms can be seen around the Tidal Basin. It is also when the National Cherry Blossom Festival takes place throughout the city to commemorate the gift of the Japanese cherry blossom trees, and to honor American and Japanese cultures, and friendships between the two countries.

During the four years under the Trump administration, Washington, D.C. had witnessed chaos and turmoil created by no one other than the president himself. Most notably was the Black Lives Matter (BLM) protest Trump violently disrupted on June 1, 2020 and the incursion of the U.S. Capitol by a mob of Trump's supporters on January 6, 2021.

I never forgot the day on June 1, 2020 when Trump ordered federal law enforcement to fire pepper spray and rubber bullets at peaceful protesters to clear a path for him to stride from the White House to St. John's Episcopal Church for a photo-op. Standing in front of the historic church but never going inside, Trump held up a Bible and posed for the photo just minutes after the U.S. and military police forcefully attacked and drove protestors out of Lafayette Square.

As Michelle and I were watching in dismay the event unfolding on our TV screen at home, I received a text message from Nikki. She was in Washington D.C. and was participating in the protest with her friends to demand justice for George Floyd, a 46-year-old African American who was killed by Minneapolis police officer Derek Chauvin on May 25 by kneeling on his neck for nine minutes. Nikki texted she was with her friends and that people were kneeling on their knees as a form of peaceful protest when suddenly the police used tear gas, and other riot control tactics, including flash-bangs and rubber bullets fired at protesters to push them out forcefully from Lafayette Square and surrounding streets. Fortunately, she and her friends were not hurt since they were in the back of the crowd, but it was a scary experience for them, nevertheless.

During the three days that preceded this event, the protests were mostly peaceful during the day. The protesters were a young and diverse group of people who called for an end to police brutality and racial inequity. At night, however, there was random violence and destruction throughout the city that seemed to be carried out or incited by a different group of people. The night before June 1, stores were looted and cars were set ablaze. Near the White House, a small fire was set in the basement of St. John's Church. Trump and his family were staying in a secured bunker in the White House where he repeatedly tweeted out messages criticizing state and local leadership as "weak" and vowing to use force "never seen before" to "dominate" the streets of Washington, D.C.

On June 1, Attorney General Bill Barr ordered U.S. marshals and federal agents from various law enforcement agencies to increase their numbers on D.C. streets by nightfall. That evening, Secret Service officers, SWAT police officers, officers from U.S. Park Police with shields on horseback, D.C. National Guard, and Air National Guard members carried shields with the words "military police," and U.S. marshals wearing camouflage came out on full force to crush the protesters. But the crowd on that day was peaceful. Nikki said she saw people were dancing on the street, a woman was playing her guitar, people with families and small children were walking among the protesters. At St. John's church, a pastor was handing out bottled waters to people.

It was a stark contrast to the protesters on January 6, 2021 who were mostly white and carried Trump, Confederate, and other extremist groups' flags and were armed with a variety of weapons such as pepper spray, stun guns, baseball bats, batons, and flagpoles wielded as clubs. The police found pipe bombs planted by the headquarters of the Democratic and Republican parties the night before. The mob included members of the Proud Boys, the armed civilian group Oath Keepers, and QAnon believers, a far-right movement of people who believes in conspiracy theories that allege the world is run by a cabal of Satan-worshipping pedophiles. They came to Washington D.C. by the tens of thousands to support Donald Trump, who for weeks, had urged his supporters to show up for a protest he promised "will be wild."

During his speech that day, Trump called on his supporters to march down to the Capitol to overturn an election he had repeatedly and falsely claimed was stolen from him. This time, there were no federal police or any federal agents to protect the U.S. Capitol. The day before, the Sergeants at Arms had denied the Chief of Capitol Police's request to call in the D.C. National Guards. It was up to the Capitol Police to protect lawmakers.

Several hundred of Trump's supporters charged inside the Capitol and attacked Capitol Police officers. I cringed when I saw the yellow flag of the Republic of Vietnam among those flying above the steps of the U.S. Capitol; it was the action of a few bad apples and certainly not a representation of all Vietnamese Americans regarding peaceful protest and respect for the constitution of the U.S. Videos and photos showed violent struggles between the mob and out-manned officers. The rioters used plastic riot shields to break through the windows and climb inside the building. A woman was fatally shot by a Capitol Police officer while trying to climb through one window. Many police officers were injured while physically engaging with protesters. One officer, Brian D. Sicknick, died after being injured. Capitol Police had to rush lawmakers to a secured chamber to protect them against the mob.

After the insurrection, over one hundred police officers were injured, five people died and over 500 people have now been charged for their roles in the riot that day. Trump called the rioters "patriots", "tremendous", "great," and "peaceful people."

Living in the Washington D.C. area for almost forty-five years, I've seen the city survive the Reagan's assassination attempt, the September 11 attack, the anthrax threat, and the "D.C. Sniper," but the Capitol insurrection felt surreal and unprecedented. Watching it on TV, I felt like I was watching democracy being attacked. It seemed inconceivable; democracy has never felt so fragile. Under Joe Biden's administration, normalcy slowly returned to Washington D.C., but political division, misinformation about the pandemic, and the Big Lie about the election remain a threat to the democracy of the U.S. as never before.

THE ENDLESS SUMMER

It's hard to believe that it has already been almost two years since the pandemic started, and we are still nowhere close to getting back to normal. Even the Spanish Flu, as deadly as it was, only lasted about two years. In July 2021, we thought we had finally beaten the virus, but the recent surge of Covid-19 infections from the highly transmissible Delta variant, because of large segments of the U.S. remaining unvaccinated appeared to make the summer of 2021 another long summer.

Last year, as the number of infections and deaths increased across the country, many county and state governments had to implement lockdown measures to control the spread of the virus. During the first couple of months, I actually enjoyed the stay-at-home order. Although I had been retired about two years before the pandemic, but it felt different. The roads were empty with no traffic; I could smell the fresh air for the first time in a while, and the price of gasoline had gone down to almost two dollars a gallon, since no one was driving anywhere. When I took a walk around our neighborhood, I could stop to look and smell the beautiful flowers on the side of the road. Suddenly, I appreciated the little things that I had taken for granted before; from food and water to hand soap and toilet paper, among others. Our family dinners had become meaningful again as we no longer went out to eat and could actually sit down to have dinner together. We were more frugal with our food and other necessities, and we cared more about our environment. Money did not seem to be important as our little world no longer revolved around it, and we took better care of ourselves since our lives were never more precious. For a little while I thought, "Isn't this a wonderful world?"

The wonder, however, did not last long as many people began to oppose the stay-at-home orders; they claimed their freedom was being infringed upon. It did not help when the president downplayed the risks of the deadly virus, and seemed to do everything he could to spread it by mocking people who wore masks, holding mass rallies, and calling for officials to "liberate" states amid protests over stay-at-home orders aimed at stemming the spread of Covid-19. Then came the killing of George Floyd in Minneapolis, which sparked protests across the U.S. and over 2,000 cities and towns in over 60 countries. It seemed the pandemic and the civil unrest had turned the Summer of 2020 into the longest summer I had ever seen in my forty-five years of living in the U.S.

For children, the days were even longer, as they could not go to summer camps or to the beaches. Our daughters have grown up now, but they felt the same way; after long working hours there were long hours and long weekends inside and around the house. We could go nowhere for a family vacation as the pandemic was ravaging across the country. We had cancelled a cruise trip to Alaska and abandoned our plan to visit the Grand Canyon, which my wife had long wanted to do.

Since we were going to be stuck at home for the foreseeable future, we decided to replace and upgrade our deck, and put in a patio so we could enjoy our back yard. In the morning, when the weather was not too hot, I could sit on our deck and enjoy a cup of coffee while reading a book or working on my laptop, watching the sun slowly rise above the Cypress trees. Sometimes our neighbor's cat would wander onto our deck and lazily stretch out under the sunrays. We also planted a row of red azaleas around the deck and some rhododendrons by the new patio and a new Crepe Myrtle tree. I wanted our house to become a summer place for us to enjoy the outdoors at home.

The long and warm summer afternoons also brought back memories of the song "A Summer Place" which I heard every afternoon on the radio in the house where I grew up in Saigon. Like the title song in the 1966 album "La Maison où J'ai Grandi" of Francoise Hardy, I often wondered whether that house of my childhood would still be there one day when I came back. Would the trees that my maternal grandfather planted for my mother still be there, or would they all be gone? The house, the trees and the people too? We had made a plan to go back to Saigon, so that our daughters could get to know our birthplace and see the house where I grew up. But the pandemic changed everything, so we had to hit pause on our plans and our lives.

When I take a trip down memory lane, I remember the past summers when our daughters were still young, in which we would drive to the Outer Banks in North Carolina almost every year for vacation. We usually rented a cottage near the beach but away from the crowds where we could enjoy the ocean without a lot of noise. I liked to listen to the sound of the crashing waves, as it took my mind off the problems and the busy work schedule I had back in Washington, D.C. My wife and the girls loved to swim in the ocean and could easily spend a whole day swimming while I preferred to jump the waves and then go sit on the beach to read a book or listen to the chansons of my favorite French singer, Christophe, on my iPod. I liked to listen to many of his songs such as "J'ai entendu la mer," "Nue comme la mer," "Océan d'amour," and his breakout song "Aline" while at the beach because they all have something to do with the ocean. Christophe was one of the most celebrated French pop singers during the sixties and seventies. In April 2020, he tested positive with coronavirus and later died of lung disease complication. He was 74. Upon learning of his death, France's Minister of Culture Franck Riester tweeted: "His words, his melodies and his voice transported us and moved us. Without Christophe, the French chanson has lost part of its soul, but the blue bittersweetness of his songs is indelible."

When we were tired of the beaches, we would go see the lighthouses, and visit The Wright Brothers National Memorial in Kill Devil Hills, as well as the sand dunes where the brothers attempted the world's first successful self-propelled flight in 1903. The Outer Banks are a stretch of islands about 200 miles long, one of America's oldest unsolved mysteries, "The Lost Colony" took place on Roanoke Island of the Outer Banks in 1587. It would have been the first permanent English colony in the New World if the settlers did not disappear because of unknown circumstances.

The Outer Banks is also the location of where "Nights in Rodanthe" was filmed based on a novel of the same name by Nicholas Sparks. My wife is a devoted fan of the author and after watching the movie, she wanted to see the Rodanthe Inn. So, one year during Courtney's spring break, we drove to the Outer Banks and to the village of Rodanthe on Hatteras Island. It was a rather cold day in early April, and there were few people on the island. We stopped by a restaurant in a small shopping mall to have lunch and ask for directions. The place was empty, as this time of the year it was out of season, but it was a pleasant restaurant with a perfect view of the Atlantic Ocean. We picked a table outside so that we could enjoy the fresh air and ocean view. The waitress was a middle-aged lady who had the looks of a person who has lived in a beach town all her life; tan with shaggy blond hair and her eyes were as blue as the sea. I noticed when she handed us the menus, her hands looked rough like those belonging to people who do labor work. I asked her what she would recommend for lunch. She said, "Crab cake for sure!" It turned out to be the best crab cake we ever had. The portion was generous, with fries and coleslaw on the sides. I asked her for directions to the Rodanthe Inn. As we were the only customers

there, she sat down and drew a little map on the napkin
for us. She told us that when the crew came to the village
to do the filming of "Nights in Rodanthe", everyone came
out to see Richard Gere and Diane Lane. She could even
get a picture of herself snapped with the actor.

After lunch, we followed the map and found the
four-story hotel by the sea. It looked exactly like how it
did in the movie, except it was closer in land, and not
right on the beach as it was in the movie. The waitress
told us that the hotel was sold to a new owner, so it was
considered private property now, therefore we could not
go inside for a tour. All we could do was standing outside
and take some pictures.

And some years, to keep the girls from getting bored
during the summer, we drove to Myrtle Beach in South
Carolina one year, then to Ocean City, or Virginia Beach
the next. During the weekends, we would go to the Fish
Market in D.C. or drive to Point Lookout State Park in
Maryland to buy blue crabs in the bushel from the
fishermen, and we would just eat them until our fingers
were sore from cracking and pulling the meat from the
shells.

My most memorable vacation was perhaps in 1995,
when Nikki was about two-years-old. We flew to Cancun,
Mexico, for a vacation. It was our first trip outside of the
United States since Nikki was born. Our adventure began
as soon as we got out of Cancun International Airport. It
was getting dark, and I was busy checking out a rental car
in the parking lot when a local boy snatched one of our
bags and ran toward the terminal. By natural reaction, I
ran after the thief and chased him around the airport.
When I was about to catch up with him, he dropped the

bag and ran away. In retrospect, although I was lucky to get our bag back, I would not have done it again, especially when we were in a foreign country like Mexico.

By the time we got out of the airport, I worried about our safety, as the road was totally dark. At the time, the road from the airport to the hotel zone was not completely paved and well lit. Fortunately, it was only about a twenty-minute drive to our hotel, and we made it there with no incidents.

The next day, when we had just gotten out of the hotel, we were greeted by an army of salespeople trying to pressure us to buy a tour. We felt easily overwhelmed with all the different prices and packages that were printed on colorful brochures. I decided to go with a young man with a simple package handwritten on a piece of cardboard that read:

"Exclusive Private Tour: Water taxi + snorkeling + swimming at sandy beach + lunch."

It was simple enough advertising that I could understand, with a considerably lower price than the other, fancier tours. The young tour guide led us to a small boat with an outboard motor installed in the back.

"Jesus!" I exclaimed silently.

I did not expect to see a yacht, but I thought the boat was a little small and unimpressive. I hesitated for a moment as my wife was pulling my shirt and whispering,

"Is it ok? Should we go with the others?"

While I had not decided of what to do, the tour guide said,

"It's okay, please go on the boat. You will have a good time."

I looked at our tour guide; he looked like a nice young fellow, so I said,

"Okay, let's go amigo!"

He promised us he would take us to a beautiful location with clear blue water where we could swim, go snorkeling, and see the fish. After taking a boat tour along the beaches, he took us to a location that seemed to be in the middle of the ocean, yet the water was shallow enough that we could touch the bottom with our feet. He was right; it was a perfect spot for snorkeling, as the sea was warm with translucent water, and there were almost no waves or currents. We could even see colorful tropical fish and some coral reefs under the water. While we enjoyed swimming and watching the fish, our guide sat and waited on the boat. After a while, he said he needed to go do something in which I could not make out exactly of what he said. All I heard was that he would come back to pick us up. Without thinking I replied, "Okay."

After he was gone, I suddenly realized that all of our clothes and belongings, including money, were on the boat. My wife asked worryingly;

"What happens if he does not come back?"

"He would not do that!" I said in a not very confident tone.

I was actually worried, but I did not want my wife to panic. I assured her that our tour guide was a nice and honest young man; he would never leave us stranded in the middle of the ocean like that, especially when we had a baby with us. Still, the anxiety kept us from enjoying the ocean afterward.

I do not remember how long we waited since I did not have a watch (it was inside my backpack which I left on the boat), but it seemed like it had been a long time when we finally heard a motor from afar. We looked around but saw nothing, then as the noise got louder and closer, we saw the boat and our tour guide coming toward us. We all let out an enormous sigh of relief. I told him I thought he had forgotten about us. He just laughed and said he went out to get our lunch.

"Lunch?" I asked.

He pointed to a bucket on the boat with about a dozen of fish inside and said:

"That's your lunch!"

"That's our lunch per the 'exclusive' package?"

"Si, señor"

Apparently, he left us to go fishing to find food for our lunch. It never occurred to me to ask him what would have happened to our "exclusive lunch" if he could not catch any fish. In any case, we were happy to see him return. He took us to a nearby beach where the local people lived. He told us we could go swimming or hang out at the beach while he prepared our lunch.

When we came back from the beach, our tour guide was grilling the fish on an open flame that he had set up near the beach. On a nearby picnic table, he had laid out green banana leaves with some steamed rice he just cooked for us. There were no utensils, so we must eat by hand. The lunch was actually very good, perhaps because we were hungry after a long day of swimming in the ocean.

After all the excitement, we thought the Cancun vacation was overall a fun adventure, albeit with a little of suspense. Since then, we have come back to Cancun several times, but we stayed mostly within the resorts or went with a group rather than venturing out on our own.

Summers used to always be a busy time for us when our daughters were still young, as we had to book vacation for the entire family and find summer camps for the girls; with these activities, three months seemed to fly by quickly. All of this seems to be in the distant past, as the girls have now grown up.

When Courtney graduated from college in 2019, we booked a week-long Greek Isle cruise. She wanted to go to Greece since she had already been to Paris in 2012 with us when Nikki finished high school. Our cruise started in Venice, Italy, and included ports of call in Montenegro, Dubrovnik, Santorini and Olympia. It was almost a perfect vacation; while we were eating lunch in a restaurant in Santorini, we checked our messages on our phones, and learned that Michelle's father had just passed away. The sad news brought a somber mood for the rest of our trip. Before we went on the trip, we knew that day would eventually come, but we did not know when, and when it happened, it still brought shock and sadness.

We were the sandwich generation - middle-aged people who have to care for young children and aging parents at the same time. I had struggled to go through that period during the late nineties when my mother suffered a stroke, and we had to take turns to take care of her while trying to raise our children. When she died, there was a lot of sadness and tears, but life had to go on.

Recently, my friend Hugh, who had moved to Australia but just moved back to the U.S., said that as we are getting older, we begin to lose more family members and friends. The problem now, though, is that the world is in a different place; the pandemic threatens to throw the evolution of human life cycle off balance. It does not matter whether you are young or old; you could be affected regardless. The pandemic will eventually end just like anything else in life because nothing lasts forever - however good or bad. Nonetheless, I believe the world will never be the same again. Similar to the changes we saw after the September 11 attack, but the changes after the pandemic will be more profound. Society as a whole has already changed in the way people live, work, conduct business, and interact with one another. People will spend more time outdoors and be more aware of the environment. The pandemic should serve as a wake-up call and a powerful reminder for effective governments committed to global cooperation in health and the common good of humanity before it is too late.

In June 2021, we took a brief vacation to go to the Outer Banks. We desperately needed to go somewhere after more than a year of staying inside our house. We also needed to feel safe, and nothing was better than the place we were familiar with and had been to before. When we were at the Outer Banks, the beach was not as crowded as during normal times, but I liked it that way. Sitting at the beach, I closed my eyes and listened to the sound of the ocean calling, and imagined the music of Christophe as it was playing in my head.

(L-R) Nikki, Courtney, and Michelle, Outer Banks, North Carolina, Circa 2001 *(Do Family Archives)*

(L-R) Courtney, Michelle, and Nikki, Outer Banks, North Carolina, Circa 2009 *(Do Family Archives)*

Courtney & Michelle, Rodanthe Inn,
Hatteras Island, North Carolina
(Do Family Archives)

Me, Courtney, Nikki and Michelle
(Do Family Archives)

ACKNOWLEDGMENTS

Writing a book is both a challenging and rewarding process which would not be possible without the help and support of many people working behind-the-scenes.

Specifically, I want to thank Emily Weisenberger, who graciously agreed to help review the manuscript, and provided excellent comments and suggestions regarding the content and structure that made this a better book than I would have imagined.

I also want to thank my daughters; Nikki for reading and reviewing the chapters despite her busy schedule, as she was completing her Master's degree at George Washington University and Courtney for her work with the book cover design.

My friends and former colleagues for reading the manuscript and providing valuable feedbacks: Jim Fitzsimmons for his candid reviews and comments, Hugh Jordan who shared his personal stories and thoughts, and

Brian Lutz who kept emailing and asking me to send him the next story to read.

I am grateful to Barbara Cook for sending our priceless photos with her and Joe during their visit to our house in Chantilly. Your friendship and kindness throughout all the years are special and you always have a place in our hearts.

I am also grateful to former SVN lieutenant and chief engineer of HQ 402, Cao The Hung, for talking to me on the phone about the ship and granting me the right to use the photos of HQ 402 in this book.

NOTES

[1] Buổi sáng mai hôm ấy, một buổi mai đầy sương thu và gió lạnh. Mẹ tôi âu yếm nắm tay tôi dẫn đi trên con đường làng dài và hẹp. Con đường này tôi đã quen đi lại lắm lần, nhưng lần này tự nhiên tôi thấy lạ. Cảnh vật chung quanh tôi đều thay đổi, vì chính lòng tôi đang có sự thay đổi lớn: Hôm nay tôi đi học...

[2] Hanoi Mayor Dismissed, The New York Times Archives August 2, 1954

[3] War in Vietnam (1945-1946) | Military Wiki | Fandom

[4] 1954 Geneva Conference, *https://en.wikipidia.org/wiki/1954_Geneva_Conference*

[5] Mark Moyar, *Triumph Forsaken, The Vietnam War 1954-1965 pp 217*

[6] Mark Moyar, *Triumph Forsaken, The Vietnam War 1954-1965 pp 220-221*

[7] Massacre at Huế | Military Wiki | Fandom (wikia.org)

[8] Mark Moyar, *Triumph Forsaken, The Vietnam War 1954-1965 pp 214-215*

[9] Cambridge University Press, 22 June 2017, *Cultivating Subjects: Opium and rule in post-colonial Vietnam.*

[10] Cambridge University Press, 22 June 2017, *Cultivating Subjects: Opium and rule in post-colonial Vietnam.*

[11] Cambridge University Press, 22 June 2017, *Cultivating Subjects: Opium and rule in post-colonial Vietnam.*

[12] Drug Use in the American Army in the Vietnam War (ukessays.com)

[13] Kuzmarov J. *The Myth of the Addicted Army: Vietnam and the Modern War on Drugs*

[14] Lam Phương, Ngày Hạnh Phúc
Ngày hôm nay thanh thanh
Gió đưa cành mơn man tà áo
Làn mây xanh vây quanh
ánh vừng hồng chiếu xuống niềm tin
Đàn chim non tung tăng
như đón chào ngày vui thế gian
Chúc ai tìm được bến mơ ...

[15] Hoàng Giác, Ngày Về
Tung cánh chim tìm về tổ ấm
nơi sống bao ngày giờ đằm thắm
nhớ phút chia ly, ngại ngùng bước chân đi
luyến tiếc bao ngày xanh...

[16] Nguyễn Hiền & Nhật Bằng, Về Đây Anh

Người ơi ! Nước Nam của người Việt Nam
Vì đâu oán tranh để lòng nát tan
Đây Bến Hải là nơi ngăn cách đôi tình
Đứng lên tìm chốn yên vui thanh bình

Người ơi ! sống chi cuộc đời thương đau
Về đây áo cơm đùm bọc lấy nhau
Đây nỗi lòng người dân tha thiết mong chờ
Cớ sao người vẫn đang tâm thờ ơ

Người về đây sống vui đời thắm tươi
Miền tự do đắp xây cho muôn đời
Nhịp cầu mến thương gieo vương ngàn nơi
Xuân thanh bình rộn ràng muôn lòng trai

Người ơi ước mong ngày tàn chinh chiến
Để toàn dân sống trong cuộc đời ấm êm
Ta nhắn gửi về nơi quê cũ xa vời
Hỡi ai lạc bước mau quay về đây

[17] Pdoggbiker, May 8, 2018, U.S. Ship Rescued South
Vietnam's Navy after Saigon Fell – CherriesWriter –
Vietnam War website

[18] Rory Kennedy, Last Days in Vietnam, 2014
Documentary

[19] U.S. Naval Base Subic Bay - Wikipedia

[20] Frank Snepp, Decent Interval, 1977

[21] 10 Disturbing Facts About Poverty in Panama - The
Borgen Project

[22] John Perkins, The New Confessions of an Economic Hit Man, February 9, 2016

[23] 1993 World Trade Center bombing - Wikipedia

Outer Banks, North Carolina, Summer 2021
(Author's Collection)